ZEN

IS

DEVELOPMENT

BY

THOMAS SKEAD

ZEN IS DEVELOPMENT

BY

THOMAS SKEAD

REVISED EDITION 2023

REPUBLISHED BY:
GOORAGANG PUBLICATIONS
ABN: 77 845 063 813

First published November 1996
Copyright © Thomas Skead

All Rights Reserved

No part of this book may be reproduced or utilised in any form or by any means electronic, photographic or mechanical without permission from the publisher.

ISBN 978-0-6453599-1-6

ACKNOWLEDGEMENTS

I would like to acknowledge assistance with editing, formatting and overall support from the back office team.

To my friends Kumudu and Ed Wright for focusing my attention on American poet Walt Whitman.

For my sister Margaret who challenged me to support a much wider group of readers.

For my wife Pauline who shines from the heart of this.

In a single breath
Joshu's "Wu"!

Readers!

Zen!

The word you'll have noticed being used in many ways.
As a shorter word for Buddist meditating, it is part of that religion going back two and a half millenia.
It is important right now, because people are falling away from dualist beliefs that are built on supernaturalism.
This collection is put before you — that a religious life is still there in a quiet but expanding manner.
Many find that they have a closer experience to religion than they have always known.
There are many leads here to follow to other teachers and many viewpoints you might see.

A Foreword from the Author
25 years later 1pm Saturday
March 2022

Looking more closely at each section of this collection against the whole, I am aware it is not a book. It is a collection of essays from the middle part of my life.

Because I developed gradually against the cultural winds and searched widely for viewpoint, the writing spans decades.

Eventually the realisation became Buddhist with an established 'Way' that even had an allegorical framework in pictures that existed in the East over many centuries.

While it is arranged for steps of direction, each reader seems to find their interest — from an angry child who feels mislead, to the man who enjoys 'ordinary'.

Some of the essays will be irrelevant and confusing and not for them, and, others might learn from my mistakes.

Yes, the ten development sections represent The 'Ten Ox-Herding Pictures' as allegorical stages that were originally devised and evolved in rural China. See Pai Chang (720 – 814 AD). The beginnings of this came when the blue-eyed monk from India arrived in China much earlier. circa 520 AD.

Via Japan, Korea, Thailand, Vietnam it has been offered to The West. Now, the tenth picture of bringing it back to 'The Marketplace' has never been more necessary. The viewpoints of teachers of Buddhist living were there for centuries. More recently Europe and North America joined the sharing adaptive learning. We are indebted to them for maturing cultures with their legends and original confrontations with the nature of The Universe.

Yet at the current time we have fires, floods, fevers, and war; it is necessary to find new adaptations for humankind, and other beings on the globe.

Among the searchers there are quite a few whose development is well on its way. They know its nature and its union, and have that lit up. Where to now?

For them, the last half of Zen Is Development has organised pieces and different print. More than reading fodder, they are stimulants to thinking, or provocative reflection steps you can hold while you take the next jump.

Where to position themselves, take their bodies, communicate to others, leave habits of thought, new direction, how and when?
They are looking for the very challenges and reminders that are around in Development 6 to 8; and I still suggest that some might want to read the whole volume from indirect starts.

In Development three and four you may be bored by my mistakes, jump to things that move vaguely, my wrong chases, or my wordy explanations that might be awry, or, my missing intuition. So, here's hoping that I might prevent the reader being distracted as I was.

'Development one and two' are about a primary school child who does not accept his culture and rejects its effects. At eight years of age, he doesn't realise it is dualistic cultures and their power that he is taking on.

As to supporting the Introduction 'backwards', I am adding that there are numerous places in it where it might be commenced to suit a wide range of people. There are traps, such as thinking you are in six when an earlier one is appropriate, or, leaving seven out altogether.

My experience is that the people who ask questions and are often becoming dismayed about many possible directions of personal life, find new directions of thought, and are stimulated to look for more.

But to focus on 'the ox herders' by numbers' or as 'an attainment' creates obstacles, on the other hand a variety of viewpoints enhances your journey.

I saw the trap of this use of the written word, hence my not drawing attention in that direction in the original book.

I have more confidence in the younger people of today, but, realise it could still get under the ox's feet. Notice how the words become sparse and simpler towards the end, and how words might cloud the way of 'seeing'.

a personal journey through
allegorical ox-herding imagery

INDEX

Development I — 1
    Enough I — 2
    The Stories — 3
    Fear — 5
    "Darwin or the Bush!" — 7
    Kipling or Khayam — 9

Development II — 10
    Fragmentation — 11
    The anatomy of service — 13
    Unsheltered — 15
    Abrupt transition — 16
    Teilhard — 18
    … TO LISTEN TO THE SOUND … — 20
    'The other side of The World' — 24
    'Wuthering depths' — 25
    'Boundaries' — 27
    Jung and 'I' — 29
    Not the true Tao — 32

Development III — 34
    Zen in the country — 35
    The Buddha — 38
    Haiku — 42
    'At the traffic lights' — 43
    The Neuronal Net — 45
    'Mr Lincoln is in bloom' — 46
    Quality — 48
    'Novice or Clown?' — 50
    To sit effectively — 56
    'Monkey' — 58
    Koan — 59
    'Encounter with a goose' — 60
    'A cow calling faintly' — 62

'The soles of my shoes?'	69
The air I breathe	70
The ridge pole?	72

Development IV — 74

Bewildered goose	75
Residues of ignorance	77
The wheel of life	78
"May 'The Force' be with you."	80
"Zazen — nothing in it?"	81
The one bright pearl	83
Its apparent form	84
Neither positive nor negative	85
'Sunyatta'	86
"... as the vein of gold goes"	87
"... and nothing else"	88
'The Way'	89
Karma?	90
Practical zen	92
Pulsars and planets	94
Identity	96
Two American novels	98
Feelings and The Middle Way	101
Shikan taza	102
Utstein Kloster	103

Development V — 105

Around a small star	106
The Tao	108
The wriggling eel	110
Rage and Reality	111
The House in the garden	113
The view from zazen	114
"Resistance is grief: grief is resistance"	116
Sitting zen	118

Development VI — 120

Yes	121
Replenishment	122
The transmutation of 'I'	127
On illusions	130
Time/change maps	133
Change	136
"The barking of the two-legged dog."	137
The inevitable koan	139
Without vision of goose or bottle	144
'Arrow, stick or hint?'	146
Fear of Seeing	147
'I': adaptive illusion and malign temptation.	148
If interested in Jesus	150
The confused scribe?	151
'The Sound'	152
Jesus enlightened?	153
The Gnostics	156
Brahma	158
"God is a verb."	160
Many enlightened?	162
Buddhism as a philosophy	164
Finding 'a way'	166
The clothes of 'seeing'	167

Development VII — 168

The raft	169
Get up! Know your face.	170
The shackled self	171
… such a creature	173
The Noble Eightfold Path	178
Salvation	181
Pain	183
The uses of enlightenment	184

The ethics of oneness	186
"Original love"	189
Becoming	191
Enough II	192
Implications	193
What comes 'next'?	197
'... and the politics'	199
"Is it done with ... ?"	201

Development VIII — 202

The Shadows	203
Rest and comfort	204
le weekend	207
Roles or the real thing?	209
"No bells ring ... "	210
She knows there is nothing else.	211
... to look through the luggage	212
... is	214
Doing	215

Development IX — 216

... all there is anyway	217
'The relief goes on ...'	220
Buddhas and beagles	222
Sheep tracks and rabbit dung	225

Development X — 226

Apprenticeship	227
Ordinary	230
Joshu's humour and Nansen's sword	231
The waves in Che-chiang	233
The endorphins of contentment	234
Limitation	235
The full circle	236

Partnership 237
("all this zen talk") 239

'Expressions in English'
Glossary 241

DEVELOPMENT I

ENOUGH I

For some babies the good feelings balance the others, for most of the time anyway. It is very hot in February and this year there were floods in Southern Australia.

The mother is not too anxious about babies although she is grieving for her own mother and frightened about the dangers of her world, but overall, the security is enough. The baby is one with all that, and has no language to confuse himself. He is yet to be taught to be apart from the other: the mother, other people, other species and everything else.

The Great Depression has lifted a little and his father is once again working six days a week in the State Railways. They have settled in a short street where two of his mother's aunts live. There is a tramway at one end of it and a suburban railway at the other.

In the middle of his second year, he knows about fingers (he calls them 'hingers'), toes and ears, as parts of the body that go with him wherever he goes. He is being taught that he is identified with the body and apart from all else, but the 'hingers' do a lot.

The words he is learning teach him this, as does being held up in front of the mirror. For him it is the personal pronouns: the 'I' and 'You', but it might have been 'Je' and 'Tu', or the 'Ham' (I or We) of Hindustani which, although not stating number, is still 'the subject' and separated from 'the object'.

Before anybody teaches him about his self or even individualism, it is this subject and object distinction in the structure of language that will shape his beliefs. 'Subject' and 'object' is the frame he is given to see his world. And there are all the 'thing' words too: forms made by the language that his thinking will follow.

> *In writing about 'development', English will put shape to what is being expressed. Despite the language itself distorting the message, "he", "she" and "I" will be needed to communicate the experience.*
>
> *Sometimes the richness of the English language will come to our aid with new forms and combinations to say what is needed, but it will be tested.*

THE STORIES

His mother reads to him a great deal: A.A. Milne: the poems first, the stories later. At the Congregational Sunday-School kindergarten the two-year-old hears the stories well; the Old Testament stories are most vivid. 'Joseph-of-the-many-coloured-coat' is a favourite.

He is frightened by God's demand of Abraham. And after hearing of Moses' origins a few times, he insists on telling it himself. The Good Samaritan and The Prodigal Son are strong in story and are favourites. He asks many questions to understand them further.

He is confused by the archaic expression in the King James Bible, "Suffer the little children to come unto Me". He asks about 'suffer' and suffering at home, and he is confused further. But he knows from the story that Jesus wanted to see the children and had time for them.

'School proper' comes before he is five. After six months at school, sudden changes come to his life. His sister is born early in the August; his mother is in hospital for two weeks (as was the custom).

In September, Hitler orders the invasion of Poland. His sister becomes very ill with Whooping Cough and the family are frightened for her life. Soon the war is already taking the young people away from sport, and his father's livelihood and debt payments are threatened. This alters his father's mood and creates a high level of family irritability.

At school he is elevated a class during the year, and throughout primary schooling will be stressed by his inability to cope with the maturity and strength of older classmates.

He is following the progress of the war closely, by reading the newspaper which his father brings home every evening. He is sure that it must be ended. He wants this to happen very much. This is to be done by winning it quickly.

He becomes adept at gathering the items for which the school appeals, particularly old aluminium pots and other aluminium items that he knows will be made into aeroplanes.

His family's beliefs were not typical of middle-class Melbourne. His father was brought up in a highly educated Catholic family, until the grandfather became terminally ill during the father's primary school years, and soon died. During his final illness the grandfather had explained to the father that he should not be frightened by or take literally the teachings of The Church.

Development I

The father as an adolescent left school after eighth grade and abandoned The Church.

Despite this rejection of Catholicism his father personally baptised him.
His mother had lost both her parents before he was born. She believed in "Nature" and being kind, but both she and the childless great-aunt who took the grandmother role, did not believe in God of the Christian tradition. Their lives were an example of kindness and care.

FEAR

He was quite afraid of ghosts and stories of the supernatural, and, as a younger child, had watched and waited for witches to appear from shadows in the half light of his bedroom.

At the age of seven he was as concerned about God, Heaven and Hell as he was about the new war in the Pacific. He secretly commenced evening prayers before he went to bed. One day in class he put his hands together in prayer to God: the person on the other end of his prayers was a very powerful God: supernatural, male and human, as he had been taught.

A girl scoffed at him. He was afraid of being judged and punished, and afraid of death.

In fourth class, the 'religious-instruction' teacher was a Protestant clergyman: full of warnings of death, who detailed the compliance needed to avoid graphic punishment in Hell. It was as if 'The Devil' was an abusing adult with whom he would be left. He developed a phobia of volcanoes, which was quite helpful to an Australian child well separated from volcanic activity.

But nonetheless, the activity which such preoccupation created in his mind was great. The prayers became obsessive and a ritual. His parents were not aware of them.

He looked for evidence of God in everyday life and asked about it at Sunday School. He was told about the miracle of the very calm sea and the fog during the evacuation of Dunkirk. He knew of the evacuation and accepted this.

He was preoccupied with the miracles in the New Testament and thought that the miracles were there to make the whole message believable to some people. He felt discouraged by this.

Then he asked his parents: both together at the dinner table: It was 1942: he was eight: "How do you know God is real?", was the core of his question.

The answer he got was very similar to his queries about Father Christmas some years before. Yes, it was about good things in people; it was about people trying to understand Nature, but nothing about 'a Man in the Sky', nothing extraordinary. They said they wanted him to go to Sunday School because what Jesus taught was a good way for people to live.

His Sunday School teacher, a kind young woman with a magnificent head of red hair, was sympathetic: "Because The Bible tells us what is true; four

different stories almost the same."
On both occasions he cried from deep down inside, cried quietly, not wanting them to know about the tears. They dried on his face: they were salty when he licked them later.

There he was — with a conviction, intuitive knowledge, not something he wanted or asked for, but a conviction just the same, that the story he was brought up with so far was mythical (like the myths in his father's 'Book of Myths')

He grieved for the 'after-life' lost, but also had a great sense of relief, as the ghosts and witches were gone

"Darwin or the Bush!"

But would he let it go? His reading ability drew him on, and he elected to stay at the Sunday School, but asked questions that showed his skepticism.

He was embarrassing to the Congregationals on many occasions: as a nine-year-old he questioned Elijah's methods in the great test between Baal and Yahweh, and then went on to read further where a large number of priests of Baal were put to death.

At the age of sixteen he won a prize for 'Scripture' that surprised those who were aware of his scepticism.

It was at this age that he was doing Biology at the Matriculation level, and Darwin and evolution fascinated him. He wanted to talk about it with his peers, those who would argue and struggle with epistemology in any of its forms. His view of the world shocked one close friend, as did this friend's Adventist view shock him, but they communicated through it just the same.

At University he was exposed to 'Science' more directly. He did a special subject called Scientific Method and took it very seriously. He was also aware of existentialism -- which was expressed to him as finding a personal direction in a purposeless Universe. He would not accept this.

Some of it was the arguments of his Christian friends: "Look at the trees, and yourself. Something so wonderful must have meaning?" He was aware that other people were happy holding various beliefs of their own, and aware that his own attitudes made him unacceptable to others, particularly to girls with a Christian conviction.

He was told he was an atheist. He learned that others said they were agnostics. They said that they couldn't make a conclusion about God and "the after-life", and it was not possible to know about it. Somehow this was easier and more socially acceptable. But it was a very unsatisfying position to him.

His Christian friends said that one had to have Faith, and it was Faith that led them to their trust and happiness. They saw Faith as something they had done themselves, and that by being baptised their soul was saved because of the death and resurrection of Christ. They said 'Christ' crisply.

Yet agnosticism to him seemed to be a 'giving up': better the ones who had chosen 'Faith', but himself, he would have difficulty in living with that. He would need compartments in his mind, and believing in two different ways of thinking virtually together.

Early on, he was aware that many people did this: carried contradiction with them: when he inevitably found this in himself, he would not be able to rest until he thought he had resolved the matter.

There was no identity for him in agnosticism, no acceptance of it as a position, no espousal of it: he'd have agreed that it might have described him — but he'd have preferred to be otherwise. It ate at him irritatingly — painfully.

Others said they wanted a personal philosophy that was satisfying, but it was often private and difficult to expose to testing.

And testing is what he would do. He was drawn to the idea of hypothesis: test against the evidence, discard, hypothesise again; do not gloss over any evidence that is not accounted for: experiment, be critical of the method of others: science had gripped him.

Was science itself a personal philosophy?

He reads in The Rowden White Library at the University Union: glimpses of psychoanalysis, Suttie's "Origins of Love and Hate", and became aware of the philosophers who saw a separate validity in 'the world within'.

Suttie's book made him very aware of his ambivalence to his mother, who had not handled his adolescence, including his attempts to separate, nearly as well as she had his childhood.

He appreciated that when Descartes divided body and soul, it was seen as a positive movement in the development of science and medicine, as it allowed the body and its functions to be studied, and thus led to an expansion of science. Then, he did not think of questioning Descartes premise, "I think, therefore I am."

Kipling or Khayam

After first year at the University, he works in a wholesale pharmacy warehouse for some months, then goes picking valencias and shaking sultanas in the Upper Murray region of South Australia. (They have machines that do it these days). There he learns to drive a Singer (the vehicle), begins to write poetry in more than the school exercise sense, and is introduced to Omar Khayyam.

Fitzgerald's verse is still there in memory. There was the strong sense of Now, the transitory aspect of life, the reduction of all, no matter how wise, powerful or famous to 'dust'. Omar's known vocation as a scientist, the concentration on this world: he could identify with this.

The Rubaiyat spoke for the value of subjective rather than objective time: it emphasised the death and dust commonality for man, but the birds and flowers and mornings are there, as well as some inconsistent Victorian apologies added to the irreverence.

This was absorbing: the metres reverberated like great music. The wine meant little at this rather puritanical stage of his development. Yet it was unsatisfying in just the sense that it was echoing the agnosticism that he did not accept, and embellishing the importance of experience in 'this world' without taking that idea further.

He was still looking; it was an undergraduate stage of tension, and there was great availability of energy to these ends. He was aware only generally of Buddhism, but in that awareness knew it was a teaching quite different from those developed about the God of Abraham and Moses.
He could sing:

> *"Bloomin' idol made of mud,*
> *Wot they calls the Great Gawd Budd -*
> *Plucky lot she cared for idols when I kissed 'er*
> *where she stud!"*

He knew vaguely it was Kipling and associated it with Burma and Tibet. It was the same year, 1952, that he read the Pelican edition of Christmas Humphries' 'Buddhism'.

He was aware immediately of not being put off by demands on his credulity, would have liked to understand more, yet was not consciously inspired, but ... he had a glimpse.

DEVELOPMENT II

Fragmentation

He attends the 'School of Anatomy'. There is blunt confrontation with death for which he is not well prepared. The student's tradition of acceptance of the dissecting room and it being set apart from the rest of the University is partly helpful.

The staff have a sense of the importance of dissecting the human body and a keen interest in the history of anatomical studies. There is an air of respect for the people who gave their bodies for learning, and this is balanced by the student's superficial irreverence. He is still among a group of friends who attended high-school together.

More reading at The Rowden White Library during breaks. He reads McDougall's (Duke University) three major books on psychology and Freud's 'The Ego and the Id' and is aware of the notions of 'the unconscious' and 'repression'.

It is all a recipe for distress. The 'Ego and the Id' divides experience not only into inside and outside, subject divided from object and then viewed in isolation, but thinking experience into 'conscious', 'unconscious' and 'preconscious', and that inhabited by conceptual structures expressed in the trinity of Ego, Id and Super-ego.

The latter is the aspect that deals with reality, 'the powerful urges' and a complex version of the conscience. Even the 'Ego' is largely unconscious and not related to 'the self' who has longings, is curious, dissects, and plays tennis.

So, the besieged 'Ego' is surrounded and stressed, and there is much intellectual and verbal work to understand the many forces with which it has to struggle.

He now understood the implications of repression in a limited way; that somebody who dealt with a fear of Hell by repression, would express an outward atheism, but if fear of 'eternal oblivion' or of separation from family was re- pressed, it would lead to an attraction to promises of an 'after-life'.

This was to be the beginning of some of his attention being directed to the manner in which personal experience could be divided into 'I' and 'Other'.

There were uncommon but distinct variations: Some would see their strong feelings due to The Devil, another would say "My young self" as if denying participation. Others would experience language telling them to take a certain action, or, passing judgement on an action. It might be called thinking, 'conscience' or an obsession, or even an auditory hallucination.

This was difficult enough without being subject to the impulses of an 'Id' or the pain inflicted by a 'Super Ego'.

It was evident that there were many variations of what people defined as their 'I', and whether they felt experience was part of their 'I' or separate from it. Somehow, it was what you believed was 'I' that shaped 'I'.

In this division, were those that had a separated part of themselves that didn't like 'I', or didn't accept feelings, were unhappy, distressed or depressed. The definitions of some 'I's were restricted to a small area of experience confined to most of the senses (if they were not too pleasurable), decision making, and a few permissible emotional experiences such as 'joy'.

Let this not appear too critical of Freud, because he broke cultural barriers against shining a strong light on the experience of the mental processes, and started many forms of help for people to change their neurotic defenses.

This included what was then a radical discovery: that the therapist had a profound effect on the immediate behaviour of the patient, and that factors to do with the twosome, especially the way they perceived each other, were critical to the therapy.

But Freud did not focus on 'the self' and there was little interest in it in The Fifties.

Christmas Humphries' account of Buddhism was a balance to all this. Here was effort from within to understand the nature of the self.

Understanding? This sounded familiar. Real understanding in the manner he wished? Was Humphries saying it was possible? What a contrast to Omar: seemingly pre-occupied by the fleetingness of life, leaving the discoursers, the pretenders, going to his science, his wilderness, his wine, but essentially to Mind in its broadest sense.

And yet the Buddha: Siddhartha Gautama: had that too; his concern for relief of suffering was primary: help the wounded, this is more important to the victim than the origin of the arrow.

But Buddhism also had its early religious roots with Heavens and Hells. He thought rebirth was another escape promised at the end of life; but, despite this, there was a great theme in common: the searching, the attempt to see as much as possible, and, as clearly as possible. That was what he himself was doing: trying to work it out.

The Anatomy of Service

He struggles with 'arm and leg'; the examinations in Anatomy went on over two years. It is a subject that requires different learning skills than other subjects, but he copes with this by drawing. The similarity of human anatomy and that of other animals gave him an intuitive sense of their fraternity.

Nevertheless, here was egoism at a painful stage. There were 'wants': to pass that year's examinations and go on to the next, a girl-friend, to finish being a student, to break away from parents, to be a good tennis player, and to be seen to be an adult.

It was also at that time when filling in a government form that he gave his religion as "Buddhist".

Then, despite an inner disbelief, there was National Service. Too healthy to fail the medical, he was soon aboard a train bound for 'The Army'.

While there he fired a rifle: a .303, veteran of both World Wars. He fired it five times on a rifle range — the power of its recoil surprised him; the anatomist speculated on its transmission through his pectorals, then his bones, to be dissipated through other muscles and ligaments to the earth. He knew this rifle may have killed more than once.

Whether from prejudice or moral clarity, he was for some things and against others. It then took him about three weeks to be employed in the regimental-aid-post full time.

He learned to dress infections, give out cough and diarrhoea medicines, to go on ambulance duty and give injections.

He wrote out fifty-one times: "I will not boil sharp instruments" The Sergeant counted them, and he had been aware that the Sergeant would count them. It is not surprising that he was later to be fascinated by M.A.S.H. and the Catch 22 protagonist Yossarian.

There was little time off; he rose in the dark to be ready for sick-parade and formed a pattern of daily work. Very tired, he slept soundly. When distressed he practiced relaxation/ meditation. He tried various postures. Later-on this experience was to be both useful and distracting.

At the end of his time in camp he had to choose a branch of the Citizens Military Forces.

At that time he had the opportunity to join a Psychology Unit preparing for recruiting and officer training. He was to particularly respect one of his officers, a trained scientist, who set the example of an ethical religious life as a Jew, but did this with no credit for supernaturalism. But the Army was part-time; he was returned to the dissecting room.

He studied psychology as an extra subject, and during this year and the next, his girl-friend became an important aspect of his life. This relationship seemed at times to be going well: but this was unacceptable to her father. Hurt, sad, angry: he is sent away at her family's decision. It is quite unresolved. He cannot see a way forward. His sadness about this is to last many years.

He became interested in opinion around the University stemming from the evolution of some Anglicans' view of God. 'God in the Sky' and the 'God of anything unexplainable by science' were giving way to a view of 'God being in the living world'.

He was attracted to the idea of panentheism (rather than pantheism which he equated simplistically with atheism -- he only knew about 'absolute pantheism' then) The idea of a God who wasn't out there or separate, but was part of the real world, (and the real world of Him) was a much-advanced view over the one preached to him as a child by The Congregational Church.

Even so, it seemed to make God vaguer, and as an extra — as if he'd been put in somewhere: a compromise for the sake of tradition.

It was certainly a view that would not satisfy those who wanted an eternal life, or be liked by those who came back to 'The Book'.

Universities are places of personal development, but at this stage of his studies, being a student rapidly blended with front-line work and took him away from the University.

Unsheltered

His allotted patients were ill indeed. An early one suddenly died of a thyroid crisis in the same manner as his mother was to die fourteen years later.

Death was vividly present. He built up the number of post-mortem attendances required. The 'fresh meat' image of post-mortems was traumatic on the first occasion, but he coped by attending to one of his fellow students who was fainting.

At the post-mortem of an adolescent girl who had died of kidney disease he was sad at the waste of her life, aware of 'the girl who might have been.' (This was 1954: well before routine kidney transplants)

It was at this time that one of his Christian friends told him of a Catholic priest who not only believed in 'Evolution' but believed in God being an aspect of the real world. The name was difficult to catch even though he heard it a number of times.

Birth was his next experience. It healed some of the death. Living in the Obstetric Hospital meant leaving his home again. He complained about the hospital food.

Birth was exciting: seeing the first baby born, later taking the accoucheur's role for the first time.

On one occasion, it was long before the advent of ultrasound scanning, he was commandeered at 'a peak hour' to deliver a 'still-born baby' whose twin had been born over a week earlier at Werribee: shock and delight: the little muscles flexed against the hand holding the baby's feet. A little cry came soon after. They were together: life and death.

Abrupt Transition

He is close to the end of his degree. He has a new girl-friend. At her Church he meets a young man studying to be a clergyman whom he was going to meet again.

The final examinations stood over him. It was not always easy to study. Separating from parents who did not wish it, was painful.

Then came a great transition: graduation, marriage, the hospital residency in the country, inordinate responsibility. Naively he would save everybody. Intellectually such an irresolvable attitude was obvious to him, but he still wanted to do it. He had to acquire skills requiring deft fingers; and judgement too, and at a time when he was deprived of sleep and lacking backup.

Death again, unexpected death, and responsibility for the next unexpected death that will come sooner rather than later, and work and more work: no time, no — separateness; his skills in surgery are developed as one chief is a good teacher, and, the other desperate to leave the operating theatre to smoke.

Living away from the city is satisfying to him. He will always have a positive bond with the country.

Sputnik 1 is launched; he watches from the hospital yard: the even and inexorable motion across the sky. People who laugh at his interest in the solar system and speculation about the Universe have had a setback.

He goes to another rural town, and does a trip each Monday into a remote region; his patients hailing his car, the consultation often in the shade of tree, the black bag on the bonnet of the car.

His daughter is born. Then to his first Practice as the only doctor in a small rural town where the clergyman was the young man he'd met some four years before. Again, there was hard work and the closed community, the lack of colleagues hard by, distance, and bad roads to specialist services.

The friendship with the clergyman grew by their mutual interest in the district's serious problems. This young man was always serious. They discussed tennis and their interest in pastoral work in the community: but nothing closer to 'The Everything'. That was until it came time for his first child to be baptised as an infant.

At this point he was faced with the father's role. The principal sticking point was the recitation of 'The Apostles Creed' by the parents. He said to his friend that he could not do this.

He thought about it: it was a concrete formulation developed centuries after the events of the Gospel; it would be a personal dishonesty, even though it would have been expedient to do so to please others and not draw attention to himself. He questioned too what his daughter's view of it might be one day. But, focused on his own position, he is unable to identify the heart and commonality in the beliefs of others.

After talking to his wife and his friend, it worked out better than he had expected. He stood up there, but by agreement did not recite The Creed.

The result was further discussion: he was aware he was being counselled in a professional manner, but not at all evangelised. Not many members of the clergy would have had the flexibility to talk of such issues with a sceptic without becoming defensive or rejecting.

Teilhard

At this stage, not only was he interested in how others conceived of God, but he was into time: time as a whole, time as an aspect of space-time, time as a dimension, 'subjective time' and 'objective time'. Time as a unity, a continuity, 'now and then' being a whole, but being, as he saw it in 1959, made up of a long string of 'nows' put together, the importance of right 'nows', making up a right life.

This was also the time when The New English Bible had recently been published. He read and re-read the stories he knew so well. He had a new respect for Jesus and Paul, to do with their changing the cruel Roman world: the origin of a religion that, despite its history, stood for fundamental peace.

He had heard of Pierre Teilhard de Chardin before, and, when he came up in discussion, recognised him immediately as the priest who espoused evolution and was a respected paleontologist, moreover had beliefs that were relevant to the world as it could be measured.

It was 1960 when he first borrowed some of Teilhard's works and was much encouraged by them. He didn't understand the implications of the difference between a 'something' and a process, particularly when Teilhard was talking about the process of the cosmos itself. But he did put it into his own terms, derived more from his own understanding of chemistry and atomic physics.

It went something like this: matter/energy is such that from it, has developed all this (the cosmos and the sphere of life), including you and me and the ability to think about it. That is very wonderful indeed.

He saw the suitability of all the chemical elements that fitted into living systems and the complexity of those that were yet to be understood. The long chains of carbon atoms, the cobalt atom in Vitamin B12, the iodine in thyroid hormone: but certainly, the human brain was the most complex of all — or so he thought. As he would put it: "All of it was developing in this manner because 'the stuff of the Universe' was as it was."

Teilhard, although the implications of his ideas were relatively humanistic and related to life, wrote from a much broader basis, and being a Jesuit priest leading a holy life, it seemed to be natural for him.

Not that there was a strong attraction to humanism: although he felt for those breaking away from centuries of oppression by closet theocrats taking power in other guises: this position did not help him.

And Teilhard's view of Man and his question: How will humanity develop next? He could accept this because it felt right to him, but he wasn't to understand until much later, how grief, or potential grief — the fear of going through grief, so inhibiting it, preventing all its processes, would stop a point of development.

In this instance, the point was whether he could grieve the loss of secure feelings of 'permanence', and the supposed solidity of the status quo. And, instead, to be left with the notions of change, development, impermanence? This was difficult. There were to be many points of grief in the transition to further understanding

No wonder Teilhard had troubles with the Jesuit establishment, he was teaching that change was the nature of 'The Everything', and that the process of change was to be seen and studied: a dynamic Universe, four dimensional and of developing complexity: and Teilhard was teaching this to a conservative Church who could not contain thought of this dimension.

How could they grieve their existing view to adapt to this?

> *He was aware at this time that Teilhard had been prohibited from teaching his views by his superiors in France as early as the Mid Nineteen-twenties, and that he had been prevented from publishing his works while alive. However, following Teilhard's death in 1955, there were no such constraints upon his works.*

... TO LISTEN TO THE SOUND ...

These years in country practice are marked by the dogged return of drama as he is confronted with the unexpected from all aspects of the practice. The prevention of farm accidents becomes one focus.

He encourages the young clergyman's pastoral work; during this he learns that Carl Roger's counselling model is the one his friend uses. His interest is stimulated.

During these years his two sons are born.

Then there are changes: his friend leaves for a parish in Tasmania, and he to practice on the fringe of the big city.

There — bookshops: he has Teilhard's writings on his shelves now. Teilhard shares that sense of the real and detectable Universe: the essence is about real existence; it is not somewhere else — the Universe that science can examine, and the function of that Universe, its evolution, its dynamism — ever changing.

Teilhard also writes about the biology of man, a biology without the need for an immaterial soul and connections to it: the implication is the nervous system being the home of mental and spiritual functions.

Teilhard is looking to a spiritual renewal that will fit with contemporary life and its knowledge, growth and changes. Here is a Christian who is credible; he would be the one to join with in undergraduate argument.

He has respect for this, combined with a certain scepticism that it might be an adaptation to the inevitable: an attempt to rationalise the old beliefs and adapt them to a position consistent with scientific knowledge of the time.

The garden has gradually become more important: trees, shrubs, grass and flowers come back inside his boundaries.

Lin Yutang's editing of 'The Wisdom of China' introduced him to the Tao.

He wondered how much it had lost in the translation, had a strong desire to understand it: was irritated at its 'vagueness', but was left with awareness of its strength, gentleness and sense of simplifying the passage through life.

He reads an article on Zen-training in a Daily: in particular about 'The sound of one hand clapping' being a focus for the trainees. He had heard of this before. He is amused. He thinks it is a riddle. He dismisses it with arrogant thought.

This koan ("I have asked everyone to listen to the sound of one hand.") was introduced by the master Hakuin (b 1686) during his initiative to renew koan study in the Mid-Eighteenth Century.

Unfortunately, he holds his distance, he is not teased by it. His arrogance that he understood it, contrasts with the writer's trust that there is yet more in it to see. His interpretation: that applause and appreciation, if sincere, do not have to be loud, but is nevertheless received, was at least his own.

Such powerful emotional resistance to learning new structures of thought is the great block to development. It is difficult for individuals; almost impossible for societies. It is an issue of grief: or rather the need to avoid grief at the change of the inner view of the world.

He can see this in others, but not in himself, so this is not the end of Development ii

He is reading in new areas of 'counselling'. In the middle sixties, Eric Berne has become popular with his theory of 'games' and his method of 'transactional analysis'.

This is concerned with both looking at the processes of mind and defining states of mind that perform as if:

>   the self was childlike at times,
>   a caricature of parents at times
>   and dealing with rational elements at other times;

However, in some people, these leading to the exhibition of virtually contrasting personalities, with the latent motives of one aspect driving the behaviour, when another is in the box seat

It was certainly aimed at awareness of the manner in which 'the self' exhibited various and contradictory aspects.

Berne brought out a fresh view of transactions between people; essentially the processes of two person events.
Berne's theories certainly asked further questions about the nature of 'the I in charge'. And it was a different view to that held by the general public.

Then the interest in interpersonal process went into the philosophical area in reading Martin Buber.

He is to seize Buber's view of the reality of interpersonal process and it is to influence his professional writings thereafter, but he didn't follow Buber far enough or the implications of some of Buber's views.

Yet this provided fresh illumination and merged with his counselling interests. Counselling skills for doctors became more important.

Then there was the growing influence of Carl Rogers: specific issues came from Rogers: a notion of the client's own direction in counselling having primacy, and the aim to allow experience of their feelings. Rogers enabled their awareness of the flow of biological processes in the Now.

However, he was aware early that Roger's methods were only applicable to those who had initiative, motivation and freedom from mental illness or severe personality disturbance. Indeed, the needs of such patients would be denied by over-application of Rogers' ideas about non-directive counselling.

Rogers saw problems stemming from a non-acceptance of emotional processes associated with a paralysis of initiative.

It was as if the troubled had an illusory blackboard on which was written their character and achievements, and, in light of which, they fought strongly to have their stream of experience controlled to fit with that written on the board.

Unable to own feeling experience, action from the heart was impossible. Rogers taught that the experience of feeling was 'self', and that 'self' was an experience of process rather than a view of a something/somebody.

He did not immediately accept or even understand this, but thought about and tested it against inner experience for many months. He was not to know that it was expression of Buddhist development.

Certainly, it was helpful: try it, test it, is what he did. Often the serious test of Roger's ideas was in interpersonal situations: spontaneity, owning feelings, giving up on specifications of self, becoming aware of the flow of self to find out what kind of animal he was. Rogers called it On Becoming a Person.

Had Rogers written back in the Sixties that he understood the false nature of 'I', and the process of developing a healthy self through Buddhist insight, the effects may have been different, but Rogers obviously thought that doing so was not appropriate.

Thirty years later, while valuing the therapy modes of self-psychology more than those of Rogers, he still values Roger's criteria to test patients' transition to functioning as a sufficient self.

'THE OTHER SIDE OF THE WORLD'

This could only bring about change: change in his authenticity. He sensed he was more genuine. It was as if he'd had protective shells that were not necessary any more. There was change in the balance of relationships, change in his attitude to 'change', so that he began to ask himself the question, was he addicted to change itself.

At this time, 1968, his mother died unexpectedly. He felt professionally responsible for not choosing better consultants earlier, and for not anticipating the possibility.

She had been the major influence upon him, and despite her attempts to intrude and control during his adolescence, had a bond to him that was unconditional

This bereavement was to have a profound effect on the direction of his life. The missing quality of the relationship had a strong and almost simple effect on his life and relationships that was not obvious to others. He would need to recognise and transform this process.

In 1969, he went to the other side of the world to study further. This was the beginning of a time of even greater change. A decade would pass before he would settle to take up a steady direction again.

What happened next was exposure to many other ideas, and new ways of thinking and being taught: as well as knowledge and confusion that required further processing.

'WUTHERING DEPTHS'

Living on his own in a Baker St basement his neighbours called 'Wuthering Depths' was a new experience to a man newly in touch with his feelings and flow of mental activity.

This only enhanced the distress of missing his family: one day after playing backyard cricket with the children of an acquaintance, he is overwhelmed by his feelings for many hours.

The two lines of thought he was to learn most about were not Freud but one of Freud's revisionists, Melanie Klein, and another analyst, W.R.Bion, who had turned his attention to group processes.

There were other important ones: Jung, R.D. Laing, Pierre Turquet, John Bowlby, David Malan and Donald Winnicott: the latter four were to teach him in person. Robert Gosling, the Director, taught about the work of Melanie Klein.

Klein's influence however, only develops slowly as his understanding of the implications of her work grows, and he later knows more of it from the work of Jacques.

Klein became a basic necessity, because to understand a seriously disturbed infant or young child without Klein's viewpoint is difficult indeed. Briefly what he found important about Klein's work is as follows: Klein saw the young infant's experience of the world as full of potential distress because of the strong experience of raw and undifferentiated 'quality': pains, noises, the smell of mother's milk, cold, discomfort and the sound of her calm voice — just quality.

It was chaotic because the infant could not use thinking to make sense of it. In the better experience of the infant, she saw an early reaction of splitting the chaos into the good experience and the bad. The bad could be separated off, and seen as outside. The good could be retained. As such this was more secure than chaos or bad experience, and, in the first year of life, adaptive.

As the baby grew through a good-enough experience of the mother (the 'good- enough' is Winnicott) the baby learned gradually that good and bad aspects of the world came from the same source — mostly in the same package: the mother.

With more maturity, learning about the world, including 'good-enough' experience, the child became able to accept this mixture of good and bad, better to discriminate value, and need less and less to split these aspects of the whole into two separate parts.

What the child was almost forced to learn about his own mother, he might learn about his environment, fellows and ultimately about the Universe itself. The Kleinian help for psychic pain was in treating those who were stuck between 'the goodies and baddies world' and the threat of chaos beneath, where even the good and bad split was useful.

The development was through accepting good and bad quality together through the experience of the therapy relationship. The Kleinian view was important to him as this frame of understanding helped him to tolerate complexity and seeming contradiction. Doing new things was easier, and people more interesting.

> Much he learned at the Belsize Lane clinic was not central to Development, but some of it was to facilitate the view and changes which we are following.

'Boundaries'

Wilfred Bion experienced Groups; he experienced their behaviours as a whole: he saw the group, including himself, as 'the organism' in its own right, so that even his own experience in the group was an experience of that group's life.

He saw their difficulties in going to work on a task, as they were distracted by the need for reassuring leadership, excitement, and the need to cope with threats.

Bion looked at the shared direction and complex communications as if they were expressed by the one organism. He was to the group what a psychologist was to the individual.

Bion also saw the group's perceived boundaries as illusory and often keeping it from a greater reality. That a group would have such restriction because of its 'boundary' was at first surprising, but he was to be aware of it in couples, families, religious and ethnic groups, as well as nations.

Contrasting with Bion were the others who taught about the breakdown of the unstable individual into madness, when a defective sense of boundary as to what was self and what was other brought about bizarre thought and behaviour, particularly with confusion as to whether processes were originating within the person's own nervous system or from elsewhere.

In considering schizophrenia they were talking about it as if the 'boundary issue' was a cause, rather than an effect of the illness.

During development, particularly through the transitions of childhood and adolescence, the sense of boundary from the intrusion of other's suggestion, expectations, influence and power is required for healthy development. It is necessary too for taking on mature roles in adult life.

Whatever the illusory nature of the boundary so developed, it is required for leadership and adaptive behaviour.

Donald Winnicott taught that the objects with which the child played were extensions of self, and that they became an extension of the child's inner world: here was what playing was about; you would see 'inside' the child because the events of his play and his inside events were not separable: essentially those children had to learn about 'boundary' and develop boundary perceptions and behaviours.

Yet madness could occur when the closeness of another produced a copy of their delusions as in folie á deux, or their body experienced the pain of the other's cancer or childbirth.

One lecture of Donald Winnicott's on boundaries in play (after the students got over him joking his way through an attack of serious angina) produced much conjecture about the boundaries of adults.

Was the surface of self at the limits of clothes? Were one student's boundaries where his bike wheels touched the bitumen? Was it the nervous system, the skin? Or perhaps the self was confined to the areas that integrate the functions of the cortex?

It is interesting to think of the 'rings included', and 'hair excluded', as well as all the other boundary quirks in the intuitive sense of individual definition. Fortunately the functioning mother's boundaries include her baby.

Jung and 'I'

Despite the close influence of a Jungian, he was concerned with the vagueness of some Jungian ideas; but again, was interested when Jung taught that aspects of conscious and unconscious experience were denied in definition of self: the unaccepted aspects were often seen in others, or in dreams.

Jung was also into the shared aspects of human mental activity, and not unlike Bion, saw them coming from the nature of the species, the archaic aspects of human commonality.

Jung's ideal for the self was of a self that developed as a result of further awareness of self-nature, becoming distinct, but owning common archaic aspects as well as denied opposite aspects, including a rich 'unconscious': essentially being whole.

This was an adaptation to the world, but then what?

He thought it was as if Jung wanted to give somebody (including himself) some- thing to believe in, to find a myth that worked. Jung recognised a universal need for such a myth: saying clearly that the inner experience of self coming from the unconscious, the dreams, imagination, fantasy, had a reality and validity that could change the world.

While accepting the presence and validity of deeper life, the notion of finding a myth just to complete personal development, didn't sit easily with him. But certainly, he had little conception of what the result might be in following Jung's recipe for understanding the nature of self.

One idea of Jung's that must have been accepted in more than an intellectual way, was the accepting of the male and female aspects of self: Jung's animus and anima, whether innate, or acquired through identifying with both parents.

He was searching himself too, for his own hidden hostility, destructive capacity and death wish, aspects of the unknown 'shadow' that was Jung's term for this moiety of 'the unconscious'.

He was different too in his behaviour: the most noticeable was his learning to cook, his different attitude to the way he kept his flat, and loss of much previous self-consciousness to do with how he might be perceived by others.

And male aspects of his personality his mother had not accepted, now became natural to him.

He liked Jung's notions of accepting the nature of man (what Rogers called 'isness') and adapting to essential aspects of being human. He was aware of Jung's borrowings from Eastern religions, but didn't identify it specifically with Buddhism.

At that time he was not aware of Jung's early access to some of the Nag Hammadi library either.

He was interested in the disturbances in development of self as observed through the theories of R.D.Laing, Karen Horney and Winnicott: here people imagined an ideal self they could never live up to, called it 'I', or conformed so closely to what powerful others wanted 'I' to be, that they lost their capacity to be or accept their own feeling states thus their thinking and emotions were separated, and their initiative lost.

Their confused 'pseudo self' which they accepted as 'I', distracted from a 'doing self' While he was understanding his own failure to take action, he was also to become aware of the distressing defenses of those who could only take 'action', those who only know hurt, who cannot stay with own thoughts and feelings, always defending against the hostile and rejecting image, and who can only put into unadaptive drama their self's struggles to survive.

This is what professionals call 'acting out' and it is in total contrast to the activity of the purposeful self.

Fifteen years later he was to be following all these ideas further in the work of Heinz Kohut and James Masterson.

These were years of going over issues of his own development, of painful insights and then putting these together, of confirming a different philosophy of self, becoming acquainted with his own organism.

He struggled with accepting his consciousness as an awareness of the process of being.

Then, a particular aspect of process became available: the notion that process might review other processes, or a process to develop new processes was possible, as well as a process to process that.

This was a beginning to understanding, but it was a direction taken that was to be a great help later.

This was also a time of extensive study, and it was study about human mind and behaviour, and even when his study was completed to the satisfaction of his

examiners, there was much more to be known.
In this period of study, he was to go back to neurology, to be amazed at what was known in the early Seventies that was quite unknown in the Fifties.

Neurology is a source of interest to sceptics generally; he was no exception: the classic cases who had lost a specific function of memory but retained another, interested him greatly. He met personally a woman whose stroke had wiped out her English and not her Dutch, and another man whose haemorrhage had destroyed his ability to lay down memories in language, but not for objects, faces, using tools, or finding his way.

He searched the literature for this type of understanding of brain functioning. This was further developing his scepticism and his science thinking, but subtly, a change, he found he was accepting of the believers in astrology and other 'clairvoyant' systems, if not their beliefs.

Not the True Tao

It was in 1977 that he was given a modern translation of the Tao te Ching. (It discussed the uncertainty of the book's origin in a scholarly manner) In the following year he digested it as he had Omar Khayyam twenty-five years earlier.

Man's position equated to straw dogs was provocative ('straw offerings' in other translations); the passivity at first implied was frightening, but the more he understood, the more the passivity became an illusion, because when anything required doing, it would not be resisted, it would happen.

> "and nothing remains undone"
> *Tao XXXVIII.*

It was a replacement for the Protestant shirt.

The true Tao was not the one that could be written about; and there were the images of being like water in adapting to Heaven and Earth, accepting the Tao, as must a 'straw dog' before the action of The World; as well as the detailed Way for subject and ruler — the attitude prescribed, the mode of doing and being: this was essentially bending with the wind, going the way the stream carries you - non-striving, harmony, gentleness, without desire.

While it came with an adaptive message, ethics, prescriptions for living, it was just that, or seemed just that. He wanted more; wanted to know - believe.

In 1978 he read Robert Pirsig's 'Zen and the Art of Motorcycle Maintenance'. This was most relevant to him. He was impressed by Pirsig in different ways; that he made a good book out of what must have been the most difficult of material; that the unity between classical and romantic quality was argued so lucidly; and the notion of 'stuckness', and the sense that internal combustion engines are not magic any more than is a modern computer: these as well. He read some parts of it many times.

At this time, he was testing the Taoist way of thinking in everyday life. But there was little to test against the nature of his thinking, its meaning or its direction: that was his impatience with Taoism — direction, purpose or rather the lack of them.

He certainly wanted something that was a structure in the sense of a truth, or an aspect of an overall truth. He likened life to a fast-flowing river: he wanted to look around and see where he was, but he didn't have to swim hard, and was able to float with its flow, take his feet off the bottom and learn more about what happened when he and the river moved as one.

At this point there was a new curiosity about Zen. He wanted to compare it with Taoism. He was lucky in that the first book he took hold of to satisfy his curiosity was Essays in Zen Buddhism First Series by Daisetz T. Suzuki. It was written in clear and concise English with an excellent style.

The introduction drew him on: then a bit about the crises of adolescence in the first few pages.

The painful dialogues with his Christian friends when they fell back on what was in 'The Book' had irritated him, so when in the first few pages Suzuki did away with 'holy books', he sat up and paid attention.

He liked the directness: if hungry you eat, that Zen was no verbal excursion into the transcendental. He remembered that Donald Winnicott had taught in some of the ways Suzuki was talking about: "There is no such thing as a baby!" was one example.

The salient thing that struck him early was that Zen was Buddhism.

The strange behaviour of the Zen Masters described by Suzuki was puzzling: he didn't understand it; but he was not being asked for a step of belief in something unacceptable, it was more that his curiosity was aroused.

Yes, there was a promise of calm and strength that comes from understanding, but nothing extravagant.

Taoism strongly influenced the development of this type of Buddhism, Suzuki explained, certainly it was an area to explore: there was excitement there, and puzzle rather than mystery: but not an intellectual puzzle — the key to it was 'the nature of self'; what is the self he carried around with him like?

The early masters were asking "What is it?", and he himself had struggled for decades with that question anyway. He remembered forming ideas, and then revising them completely when they didn't hold with what he knew. Not only were his own ideas changing but there was an inkling of what effect any real understanding might have on his life. There was an element of fear in beginning this, but a sense of a new direction and openness.

But he had seen something without which his very nature was incomplete: and he had the conviction it was there to be found.

DEVELOPMENT III

ZEN IN THE COUNTRY

The large window does not need a curtain or a blind: the house is well out in the country, and anyway, it faces South. In the foreground is a variegated hibiscus; about four metres away are two grevilleas, one with small vivid orange flowers, and the other, taller with red flowers. It blooms twelve months of the year; both nourish Australian honey-eaters, but one species at a time, as there are struggles for possession of such valuable real estate.

I am sitting on a plain green carpet. My left foot does not reach my right thigh, but is more resting on my right knee. One of the metallic stays in my back brace has come through the fabric and is sticking into me; the usual lower back pain is crying for attention, but there is a more insistent stretching pain in my left hip.

I remember with a smile the small boy at gymnasium class whose body did not bend or co-ordinate; it is the smile of the adult who cares for the boy back there in 1943. The laughter of the other boys is shared in my amusement at the irony now.

Consciously relaxing, I realise I will fall backwards. If the half-lotus position has this effect, the thought of learning a full-lotus is a belly laugh; it is not the back-brace, or being forty-six, it would have been similar were I sixteen or twenty-six.

A good teacher would have helped me choose an appropriate cushion and advised me on some exercises to help with the half-lotus posture. I might then have even used the two steel strips on either side of my spine to advantage.

The compromise is to sit in a straight-backed narrow typing chair with a small cushion behind my lower back. I am most encouraged by Suzuki's scholarly account of the development of zazen (sitting zen meditation) and also of his account of the Buddha finding quiet places to sit. (from the *Sutras* - Scriptures)

I am determined to explore zazen practice for many reasons; I am aware that meditation (*Sanskrit* — *dhyana*) goes back to ancient India and has been a core aid to development throughout Buddhist history.

There is confusion and clutter in my mind, with mixed shades of feeling. I know how little I understand the nature of myself; not only the nature, but how mind is, how it works. Yet I have many friends who were helped in their lives by both meditation and yoga.

I'm reminded of Descartes position; *'I think: therefore, I am'*, but I know

Buddhists were examining the elements of this premise critically two millennia before Descartes.

I knew that the other method of obtaining awareness in Zen Buddhism was meditating on koan. Both koan and zazen are first directed to understand the nature of one's self.

Koan are short questions, propositions, or even stories, encapsulating direct meaning, but in a form challenging to a mind trapped in unhelpful thoughts.

Metaphor and parable in koan are used in the communication of basic truths, and are not used simply to make the teaching more difficult. Their goal is intuitive understanding — they are an aid to shake one's view from the moulded form imposed by verbal thinking and socially accepted ideas.

The mind struggles to become the fresh view itself, and it is both the struggle and the 'becoming' that bring development.

It is intuitive perception: 'seeing', which is promoted at the expense of formal reasoning such as verbal sequences, propositions and inductive logic. That might make it easier to some.

I accepted this aspect because of all the meaning that was part of me from Winnicott's 'There is no such thing as a baby.' in my own training.

I was also aware of the Christian koan when Jesus was asked by the man about entering into the Kingdom of Heaven, and Jesus said that he would have to be as a young child to do so.

Most koan have an absurd aspect to them when taken literally or superficially. Strangely, too, if they are approached as a riddle that requires intellect, they become valueless.

Intellect is a hindrance in becoming 'as a small child', it can be a great starter when approaching other koan.

Live a koan, be a koan: that is helpful. An intellectual struggle to 'comprehend' a koan is unhelpful.

Development III

The house in the country was built on thirty-two acres. The back paddock had a rise towards the house and then fell to a creek which wound across it. There were two stands of timber of about an acre each, one of white stringy bark and the other mostly casuarina.

I bought three cows with calves only some weeks old. The boss-cow was a very large horned Hereford we called Gertie. Her daughter was named Fernanda (the correction of a mistake about her sex, when she'd only been seen from a distance and still had some umbilical cord attached).

Gertie was always the dominant cow. She arrived first when called; she ate first. She was confident, fairly trusting, healthy and substantial. She would only have to wave her horns at Rippleside — a flicking motion with her neck — and Rippleside would not approach the first leaf of hay.

Gertie's daughter Fernanda grew to be a large well-formed cow with a gentle nature and no horns to wave at the others.

From an early age Fernanda came to be given milk thistles over the fence. She liked to be handled about the face and was always relaxed and friendly. As Gertie's daughter she may not have needed to be powerful with other cows.

On the other hand, Rippleside was a cow with an eye to mischief. She had learnt to be opportunistic and to branch out on her own. If there was a slack part of the fence, she would find a way to slide through it to the vegetable garden. When the creek became dry, she got along the creek bed under the low wire and into to the house paddock.

I would be looking for what she would do next.

Development III

The Buddha

At this time my testing of Buddhism caused me to read a great deal. Much of this was about The Buddha himself.

Siddhartha was the son of a local ruler in a small Himalayan state (the Shakya people). This was in the Southern part of modern-day Nepal. It was governed as a republic by a council of local rulers.

Siddhartha's life was privileged, and his likely future was to take his father's place.

He was secluded from life outside the family compound on the order of his father, the legend has it, because there had been a prophecy that his son would be a great king or a great holy-man, and his father wanted him to become the former.

Yet, at the age of twenty-nine, he went outside, driven in a horse-drawn vehicle to a nearby settlement. In the course of his journey, he was to see a sick man, an old man, and later, a corpse and an ascetic holy-man. The effect on him produced a crisis in his development, particularly focused on the occurrence of suffering.

The prevention of suffering was to become central to him.

I often go over in my mind this phase of his development, considering what might have happened at this time.

He left his royal life, his father, his wife and young son and became what was traditionally an apprentice holy-man — a mendicant, which was essentially a beggar given over to a spiritual life and spiritual training.

This was a respected life course in that society. It is important not to have confused images with the Twentieth Century: the evidence indicates a well-organised agricultural community, politically stable, with strong religious concerns and not suffering from overpopulation.

He sought out the best of teachers and learned all they had to teach him; he found a group with highly ascetic practices, but realised that no amount of self-denial and severity of ascetic practice could itself bring satisfaction to him.

After six years, he became very determined to bring concentration and effort to complete his understanding. He bathed, then sat beneath a pipal tree (a type of fig often referred to as a bodhi or Bo tree: *bodhi* — 'truth' in the enlightened sense), determined to stay there until he gained understanding.

His companions were scornful that he had accepted a bowl of rice milk and left him. He had indeed given up extreme asceticism including starvation as a way to find spiritual truth.

Tradition has it that he was tempted, made guilty, distracted by Mara the destructive spirit.

Then after some days, he saw the morning star, got up, said that he 'no longer would seek the ridge-pole in the house', and when asked was he a Saint or a God, he said "I am awake".

With his new vision, he was very aware of the difficulties in reaching his present understanding.

Legend has it that Brahma communicated to him: There would be others "with dust across the eyes" who wanted to know, and he could help them, although it was not easy to tell or teach his experience.

Yet the impact of his person, his example, made his teaching impressive and lasting.

It was he who went into assist the disciple stricken and befouled with dysentery. He went to the murderous robber on his own. He rejected magic and the miraculous. He lived a beggar's life of simple goodness.

And this he continued through Northern India, until he retired to a grove, where he was to die in his early eighties of food-poisoning.

The Four Noble Truths were central to his teaching:

That life was suffering.

That suffering was due to desire (craving).

That defeat of desire was the key to preventing suffering.

That applying The Noble Eightfold Path was the method.
Which was:

Development III

> Right thought (views)
> Right intention (motives)
> Right speech
> Right action
> Right livelihood
> Right mindfulness
> Right effort
> Right concentration (meditation)

Now, while I could identify with the crisis elements of his development, and indeed would catch myself projecting elements of self into what he must have gone through when confronted with the sick man and the corpse, much of this was expressed in a manner I was not able to understand.

I realised it was abbreviated, that important elements were represented in the story by a short phrase. The bit about Brahma smacked of The Old Testament — the traditional bits echoed folk religions, and if it hadn't happened half a millennium before Jesus was born, I would have thought themes of The New Testament had been taken up.

The Morning Star, the Eightfold Path, the house without a ridge-pole, the old man, the sick man, the corpse and the ascetic all have their parallels in the griefs at the changing world and the developing vision of unity.

And they will recur as I struggle with them, or take a fresh view of them in a 20th Century context.

Nevertheless, the overall story of Siddhartha of the family Gautama was of development by way of all the elements of his Eightfold Path. (he is more commonly called **Shakyamuni** in Zen Buddhist circles: that is 'sage of the Shakya people')

This required effort, concentration and mindfulness towards understanding what it was all about, which brought it around to the first element 'right thought (views)' once more — a wheel of development.

But knowing that the understanding of 'the nature of self' was a way to understand the greater context, was an element I was unable to grasp.

On two occasions Rippleside was into neighbours' places — once along the creek bed, and another time between some loosened wire. She didn't tackle good fences.

My daughter Cassie and I would take Candy, the young border-collie and we would persuade Rippleside to go back the way she got out. This was relatively easy: at about fifteen metres she would keep her distance and go away from her herders.

Rippleside just branched off on her own. Gertie didn't follow her. There was cud from the morning hay to chew and good pasture at home, but Rippleside was always wanting something else. I was preoccupied with what trouble Rippleside would be in next, to the point of being teased about it.

So, I was quite dismayed when she pushed open the hayshed door. She had pulled many bales to the floor where the loose hay mixed with fresh cow dung.

When I first thought of selling her, I realised that her previous owner must have marked her out to be sold too.

Then she exposed a weakness in the back fence and found good pasture among some horses, and took a long time to return to her correct paddock when herded, but I rationalised that, as my elder son Malcolm and I repaired fences after her, the state of all the fences would eventually improve.

At this stage a visitor asked why I was a 'beef producer' who didn't eat beef. Little did he realise that there had been no turnover of stock.

That was until I drove down the gravel road at dusk to find Rippleside standing half across the road munching some roadside grass.

Not long before, a neighbour died when his car struck a horse on the road.

Rippleside was rounded up -- some special hay, the gate closed. 'A store cow'; I told myself the next property would have good fences. Her departure left a sense of regret.

But at that stage I still thought of myself as being capable of herding cows, it was easy, they'd have their worm drench, be tested for tuberculosis or brucellosis: no trouble at all.

Development III

      on effortless wings
           sea-birds wheel above the fjord
           the white mountain glows

'AT THE TRAFFIC LIGHTS'

I will tell more about reading 'Zen and the Art of Motor-cycle Maintenance'.

At one time I was most interested in the issue of apparent change of self associated with major psychiatric treatment, but also how this was reflected back to Pirsig by his son's confusion and soiling. The 'I' left by the psychiatrists was not the 'Dad' Chris had lost.

On the other hand, I was aware of Pirsig's disclaimer to represent Zen or 'Motor-cycle maintenance'. I thought his publisher had decided to paraphrase Herrigal's classic 'Zen and the Art of Archery' to have a good title.

I remembered during my first reading, noting that Pirsig wrote of his reading a philosopher and matching his own ideas with the text, and then seeing how the author's ideas would develop. I laughed as I was doing just that with him.

I heard what he was saying about the 'Now' as a film on the front of the train moving steadily.

I thought the question: How thick is that film? For experiment we make it a nanosecond (a thousand-millionth of a second): a photon might be just about to impact on a retinal cone-cell sensitive to 'red wave-lengths', but it won't reach the cell membrane for a few more nanoseconds.

Then it will be some milliseconds (thousandths of a second) before the depolarisation of its membrane would affect the ganglion and relay cells to propagate up optic nerve towards the' lateral geniculate body' of my mid-brain.

It won't affect my optic cortex just beneath the hard bone at the back of my skull, until about twenty-five milliseconds into the future, giving a tiny message: 'light — red' to add to the millions of other messages. Yet in that fraction of a second, they will register there (upside down) as a whole, and later, in a secondary visual area, be perceived as a traffic light.

The number and complexity of these required processes are unfathomable.

I am sitting in the car looking at the traffic lights. The light has been red for such a long time; I start thinking about the light. Have my tyres failed to trigger the simple computer operating the lights? How does this particular computer work, and how would they program it for right-hand turns into the highway? If it.....

There is a startling auditory sensation (reaching my cortex quickly and drawing attention) as the motorist behind me sounds his horn to indicate the light is green and I am obstructing him.

The internal questions have been fast verbal, at least at my top reading speed: they were processed at an auditory perceptual level to a verbal perceptual level then to a series of dynamic concepts. The thinking has also contained some imagined cars turning right, and has attempted to follow the designs of a traffic expert.

And this type of internal argument is very like a social discourse of a rapid and constructive kind. (Except that it has left me obstructing the traffic)

Milliseconds have turned into seconds with the verbal processing, and my neurophysiological systems that have tried hypotheses in a slapdash fashion have taken so long that the light has turned green.

There is then a 'reaction time' of about 800 milliseconds before my calf muscles bring about the acceleration to please the motorist behind.

I suppose when Pirsig talks about the 'Now', then I must ask questions taking into account what I already know about the brain processing the input: What is happening 'now'?

Is it the green light being a significant difference in my total view of the immediate environment? Is it the emotional reaction to the auditory stimulus?

There is feedback from the tendons and proprioceptors in my accelerator foot, and what I have learned previously about all the stimuli and the whole I make of them. These take time.

Somehow this 'I' is a slow character compared with the speed of some of the faster neural processes, particularly when 'I' uses internal dialogue (even at fast reading speed).

Yet, were the cursor of the mind fixed to the green light without thought or words or care for rule breakers, then it could act at a different speed.

The above story at the lights has an important element: it was a social occasion, beset with social rules about what one should do at coloured lights, and a well-understood non-verbal communication between the central characters.

The Neuronal Net

So when I think about 'now' in nanoseconds: the idea of 'I' is ridiculous, but crystals vibrate, charged particles interact countlessly in such a short time.

Certainly, a movie film takes advantage of the time delays of the optic cortex to provide it with the illusion of life-like movement from a series of still frames.

The brain is mostly fooled, except when the wheels of the covered wagons appear to go backwards.

How many illusions are there? If one wants to see it as it is, one has to see beyond the illusion, but also know the illusion intimately: — and what they are to each other; know how the magic lantern of perception works.

I go on in this fashion because I had this knowledge when I was to start zazen practice and it certainly affects many conclusions I draw, and while I revise and question neurophysiology, I also question experience or opinion that is not consistent with it.

The principal theory of the neuronal organisation that might be responsible for 'awareness', is one concerning the processes of a neuronal network working on a different time-frame from the processes which immediately organise incoming stimuli.

This can only involve some delay: an organisation that involves integration of attention, perception, learned responses (not forgetting the social) and memory.

The organisation has unique processes experienced as feeling: feeling sets the priorities of the system, provides the energy, motivation, initiative, volition, as the organism does some of what its nature determines it might do.

Such feeling gives not only internal signals, but easily recognised ones to the outside as well.

This is William James' coupling of 'stream of consciousness' with 'awareness' Late Twentieth Century version. This is a simplified neurological basis for what is being studied in neuroscience. It heralds an explosion of knowledge in the new Century.

'MR LINCOLN IS IN BLOOM'

George Engel from Rochester N.Y. became interested in how the organism survived gross pain/distress and the depression-withdrawal that ensued. He recognised the quality dimension of emotional experience and wrote about 'Anxiety and Depression-withdrawal: The Primary Affects of Unpleasure.'

The two sides of the brain are important here: the so-called non-dominant hemisphere developing an overall picture (gestalt) of what it perceives or what it expects to perceive, and then notices differences (the neighbour has cut a branch off that tree; Mr Lincoln is in bloom).

The so-called dominant hemisphere, thinking in a linear and verbal fashion, putting meaningful sounds to things and events as is required with certain social animals, the refinements of which, as far as we know, have only come in the last few hundred thousand years of our species' long evolution.

One outcome of all this neurology might seem obvious: there is no essential difference in processing, whether an incoming nerve impulse comes from the ear (cochlear), the skin of the ear-lobe, or is perceiving internal thinking process involving memory matching and telegraphic verbal thought.

They are all integrated in neural networks, and each can be selectively stopped: for example, hearing by a complete lesion of both eighth cranial nerves and ear-lobe sensation by some local anaesthetic, and short-term memory matching by destruction of certain brain tracts, including the mamillary bodies, due to a severe lack of Vitamin B1 (usually with alcohol).

Whether from within or without, thinking, sensing or remembering, it is all processed by the nervous system.

I'd heard two opinions in neurology: one says that 'mind' is the phenomenon of the brain functioning; the other that there is no such thing as 'mind', only mental processes.

Is the phenomenon of a brain functioning experienced by a something, or is this 'something' another phenomenon occurring in a more complex and sophisticated network of neurones: a process that processes the less complex processes?

New evidence from attentional research raises the hypothesis that this is a function of the cerebellar vermis.

An experiment conducted by drinking alcohol would suggest that the more complex the process the more it is vulnerable, and more easily rendered non-functioning without causing death of the organism.

Similar natural experiment occurs when nerve tissue is deprived of oxgen, glucose or other essentials for adequate functioning.

Dualists become confused at this point: in wanting the 'soul' to be a 'something', they must have it 'connected' yet invulnerable.

Whether the soul is process or structure, such natural circumstances impair it destructively. I remembered as a third-year student, being taken on our first ward round by our Dean, the legendary Panzee Wright.

The patient had suffered a stroke. Panzee remarked on the difficulty the family had to understand the loss of lifelong personal character as well as bodily function when the brain was impaired.

This knowledge was denied by the culture of 1953

I thought about it a lot. Now, the issue is basic: there are processing sytems to overview and integrate the simpler systems — to such awareness that the dreamer is awake

Development III

QUALITY

Then Pirsig's great struggle with 'quality': the unity between romantic/aesthetic quality, and technological/classical quality was so convincing that I started to enjoy putting together toys and pieces of furniture that come in kits (mostly that is).

I gained confidence with the screwdriver and the ruler, and became technical when I needed to.

I was reminded of this when considering a friend stringing his own Cello before the performance; and Medicine itself has always been at its best when the two were together.

It was a shame that Pirsig had not read Melanie Klein. Her theories are entirely about quality. Her work could be entitled 'The Ontogeny of Quality'.

Essentially, she says that Quality is primary and is differentiated from nothing/chaos, split totally to good and bad as the processes/experiences are managed by the developing infant, and then further differentiated as the infant can bear some negative quality. Yet she would see it as a biological development process.

She would have thought Pirsig's idea of quality being a unifying aspect of Religion, Art and Science as a ready extrapolation of infant life, but would have focused on the remnants of bad quality that lead to feelings of persecution and envy with resultant suffering. The search for good quality is the backbone of her psychoanalytic theory.

Another issue of Pirsig's I valued was the formulation of the notion of 'stuckness', to deliberately remain 'stuck' in thinking to prevent the mind coming to a closure too easily, and giving itself a false solution. I'd gone those ways, but explaining boldly and clearly was something much more.

I remember thinking I would have liked to have had more about Zen with Pirsig's thinking behind it. But it was that curiosity, 'stuckness', that had me reading Suzuki.

> I had noticed that the South-side neighbour's cows were not in good condition. Most of the border area was trees and scrub. It was difficult to observe their pasture. Walking in an area near the front corner of our home paddock, Candy and I came across a strange half-grown bull calf. This was an area with the best fence.

He looked up at us, ran along the fence, suddenly veering at it, leading with a foreleg below the top wire, and spread the barbed wire with a crash, bending the metal droppers that held them steady. He was back on his own side with only a few wisps of cow hair left on the wire. Concerned about his condition I telephoned the owner. She said "What cattle?"

A long story shortened: They had been rustled and dumped there. The men from the municipal pound came and took them away; saying they couldn't catch some of the young ones.

'The young ones' were four underfed and runty young Herefords about eight to ten months old, one I'd met already. We talked to the elderly owner. She wanted to sell the forty-eight acres. We accepted.

These four got through many neighbours' fences. The men at the pound said they were my responsibility.

The other neighbours now knew this too. Any attempts at herding them into the back paddock with Gertie et al were laughable. They went through fences at will. The little one hid in thick scrub, and, one time, in a neighbour's house paddock.

I noticed that she only had remnants of her right ear, and her left was torn, and hanging: old injuries; it was thought likely that she'd been attacked by dogs when she was young, as all her barb-wire-fence crossing didn't seem to hurt her vulnerable ear at all.

More complaints.

Some Australian stockmen, dogs and rough-country horses were enlisted. They rode and herded, and two runty heifers were caught after being ridden down, but the cattlemen gave up on the other two:

The young bull went through fences where the horses couldn't follow, and back through others when they'd gone through gates.

'The Little One' avoided and hid. I noticed her after the day was over. What she had done was to get through the fence and was behind Gertie and Fernanda, cautiously looking for the next danger. It was with them she was to stay

The young bull was quite unable to be caught and because of his talents could go though any paddock he wished. He did for some time, but I heard that he came to a sudden end.

Development III

'NOVICE OR CLOWN?'

sitting
hands are awkward
the old accident
the right forearm will not rotate
to the traditional position
give up hands
they could go away
until I've finished

eyes down
half closed
lean back on my brace
shuffle bottom a bit to get my back right
hands in the way
Reminds me of my hands
twenty-five years ago
I'd just given up smoking

hands
right hand holding the left
sitting here for that time
I haven't counted a figure
sitting straight
chair okay for this?
knees a little apart
feet straight
get body arranged somehow
if this chair bit is to help
beginning to see the advantages
of sitting on a cushion

the room is a problem
where?
eyes as difficult as hands
the space bar is plain grey
not distracting
hands want
the typewriter keys
my brain   not my hands
the bit that works my hands
wants to be active
won't keep them still
eyes back to space bar
want to scan

read 'Remington'
rather than stay quiet

still not counting
effort
hands
mind on my breath
"In one... Out two"
breathing faster   slower
messing up my own breathing
I got to two
One two   three four   five   six   seven   eight
  nine   ten   one   two

"they'd like to take it apart"
wandering to Tuesday

"Concentrate"
I wasn't
I was
not now "She'll ask."
"Look at their simplifications"
but one two three four five six
where to? where does this go?

One two three
four five six seven
hands again
if I could just breath ... count
without changing my breathing
worse than when you take your own pulse

***

This caricature of zazen attempts to capture the very early experience. It is very new and strange at first, difficult in purpose as well as difficult in meditation.

The mind wanders off; it can even do it to a background of steady counting. Something that is important on the day, can come into brain like a storm: that is often a sign you're concentrating your thought is succeeding, but I wasn't surprised, as the very function of emotion is to make priorities for brain processes, not only which ones occur, but what is remembered.

Development III

I did more reading as well as much sitting. Wads and wads of failures, bad habits: it is surely better to have guidance at this stage.

I had a few problem weeks when I seemed to have found an excellent way of going off to sleep.

I read how Shakyamuni had held up a lotus flower in his hands and shown it to his disciples. He had caught Mahakasyapa's eye, who had immediately 'seen' the truth. Legend has it that the truth without words was transmitted from Patriarch to Patriarch until Bodhidharma had taken it to China.

The verse:

**'A special transmission outside the Scriptures; No dependence upon words and letters;
Direct pointing to the soul of man;
Seeing into one's nature and the attainment of Buddhahood.',**

is traditionally used to affirm zen as a religion. To be less ambiguous the word 'soul' could be best rendered as 'spirit'.

On a number of times, I stopped and asked myself: What was I trying to do in zazen practice?

Then, I answered it best by saying that I was trying to quiet some of the emotionally driven thinking, to inhibit that part of my brain that thought in a linear verbal manner;

I was aware how much that part of my brain inhibited my writing poetry; there I needed images and intuitive insight first, along with music — the words last. I was criticised for not being a craftsman with words, arranging them on the page, but I did not accept this.

The verbal part of my brain I recognised as often being cumbersome and slow. I watched it sometimes; and knew it operated in different speeds or styles:

There was verbal telegraphics — a sort of shorthand where I would have a word that represented a concept — I would then make a fleeting leap to another key word — often this went side by side with intuitive processes — action too — my mentor/supervisor at the Belsize Lane clinic used to sit watching my hand gesture vigorously as we talked though a session of therapy.

Then there is the thought that goes along verbally at fastest reading rate, with jumps in between, and then there is thought that prepares to talk to somebody, even a public speaking version of that, which is rather slow.

And I'm even slower into a dictaphone as I reject words I might have said.

When I do my fast-jumping verbal thought while talking I have irritating habits of suddenly stopping in the middle of a sentence, or taking a jump, leaving out something.

On the other hand, my public speaking style is a result of me doing much thought then making interpolations. This brings a slow and sometimes disjointed result.

Yet for zazen practice I was attempting to quieten all these verbal functions. Now I was aware from Gestalt psychology and studies of left-brain function, as well as the work of George Kelly, that the brain forms a whole view of the world and is ready to notice changes — it sees these as foreground and background depending of the emotional significance is there.

This has been valuable during evolution in finding one's way around the countryside in the topography sense, finding food, looking for dangers, including enemies.

It also applies to understanding the world: its 'How'.

Kelly sees the brain not only doing this, but projecting this construction to the immediate future: as a whole picture, and rather than being in 'the now', Kelly is saying the brain is looking to the next events, the next movements, next words and how they will be responded to....

Yet these processes can be very complicated, particularly as they attempt to make sense of other people's emotional/ motivational state.

Most of this process is spontaneous and non-verbal. I questioned whether it was a resource I needed to continue when I had quietened the verbal part of my mind? Or, would this also put in much random activity and hinder me... from..... what?

Understanding the nature of my self — was one goal: putting my brain into a level of functioning that it would best be able to cope with the type of comprehension that koan obviously required, was another. Yes! I would need to stop its future anticipating too, trim the buzz of both memory and anticipation: pare it down to 'Now', however one did that.

Development III

The little herd lived peacefully. I learned a compromise language between English and 'cow'. For example, the word "More" when pronounced in the cow fashion and called loudly through cupped hands would actually make Gertie run. The fragrant leaves of Phoenix Park hay were a strong back-up to our communication.

One of the cows was very old and had lost most of her teeth and was later to die, and she was replaced by a strange cow whom we called 'The Runner'.

She was brought in by truck one evening after dark, and I didn't see her until the following day. A middling sized Hereford cow with lightly built legs, she had frightened eyes. She observed Candy and me acutely.

Fernanda ambled towards us. 'The Runner' turned and ran. She ran with quick short strides, in contrast to Gertie, whose run at the call of hay, looked like an irregular and undignified gambol.

Even when the best hay was available in the open round-up yard 'The Runner' stayed well back, ready to run. She was always very alert, and, while she generally followed Gertie, as soon as man or dog appeared she left the others and fled in her own manner.

'The Little One', on the other hand, stayed on the other side of Gertie and Fernanda, but she would go into the round-up yard for hay if nobody was around. She stayed 'little' over the years and beside Fernanda she was tiny.

What could be done if 'The Runner' or 'The Little One' needed o be tested by the Agriculture Dept or required some veterinary procedure?

The trial came when it was time for worm medicine is squirted into the side of their mouth by a 'drench gun'. 'The Runner' ran. She sensed what was going on and headed for the back fence.

'The Little One' went into the makeshift round-up yard to eat hay with the others and I quickly shut the gate.

She looked at the loose wire gate, blocking her exit, then ran at it hard, striking it at the end where a loop of wire held the upper part of the post. The wires spread as she had learned in a fast jump at fence, but this time the loop lifted off the top, and the whole thing collapsed.

She was through.

She went away and looked back, waiting for the others. I picked up the gate to keep them in.

After that we bought a substantial steel mesh gate.

When the next time came, and I pulled this strong gate shut on her, 'The Little One' slumped to a low-profile posture, was tense, alert, sized up her situation in two seconds, and suddenly jumped, launching herself at the high rail fence beside the gate.

She struck the top rail with her shoulder, and, old casuarina wood, it splintered on impact, and she virtually climbed over the second rail that was about human chin high, clearing the low barb-wire fence on the other side.

She landed without falling. Then she only ran for about twenty metres, stopped again, and looked back at us. She wasn't coming back.

There was the broken rail, otherwise it was unbelievable. The centre of the rail was soft and I was glad she hadn't jumped like that at a piece of four-b'-three.

The others soon joined her back in the paddock.

To Sit Effectively

One night, through the branches of some young eucalypts agitated by the West wind, I saw the half moon lighting a clear sky.

It seemed right. Perhaps an experience pointing where I might go in my zazen practice.

I must comment that as others seem to have trouble with their legs or their back (as I would too but for my chair and cushion), I certainly had trouble with my hands. I found it difficult to have hands that would not quiet or help my meditation. It was necessary to put them somewhere where they were a positive part of my practice, and relaxed enough.

Their getting in the way was not solved quickly. Because my old right forearm fractures did not allow the traditional position, I tried some other formal positions for them, but found I was all hands. They were a greater problem than my legs.

After some months, I found a position for them that suited me: My left hand is palm upwards and relaxed. The index and middle fingers of my right hand are together and relaxed, the hand held with the palm downward; the two fingers together then touch the left thumb near the nail.

I also found that while counting was helpful, particularly when I became the number as I counted it, I wanted to get away from the verbal element. Being conscious of the area about five centimetres below the navel was something I tried: not just that, but being conscious of the breath regularly 'arriving' there with a little motion in and out — an illusory destination for the breath that would happen anyway.

After quite some experience of sitting, I became much more conscious of my body as if I'd not given it proper attention previously. The movement of my belly with breathing seemed to be accompanied by a sense of relaxation and great freedom.

I would also be amazed by the stillness of my body and at times my thinking would be very quick in contrast to the body's stillness. There are many sensations and experiences that are described with sitting, and some 'meditation ways' encourage some of these extraordinary states; however, they come and they go, they create distraction and sometimes alarm, but like unresolved feelings arising in zazen, they develop like the weather and pass to another experience. I was to navigate these because I was focused on looking for the nature of self.

My concentration was linked to the easy but particular posture of my hands, the focus of process would be felt in my body, and I was beginning to be

refreshed. Yet I thought I was learning more about my mind
    but sitting is the body doing....

    there is continuity
    froth goes with body doing....
    froth:
    thinking
    feeling
    intuiting
    sensing
        all body doing....
           it was simply too obvious
               the air coming
                   through the nose

Yet while there were thoughts about the processes of mind, the nature of self was not encountered, however there was a sense of a new direction or rather some new skill or view: it was vague. It was as if somebody said, "You go out searching this way until you find it yourself."

The enlightened teacher
shining with happiness
in God's garden might tell
of his knowledge.

Marvelous words,

but to see this personally

with conviction,

to be first hand,

to be familiar with The Way,

it is necessary to sit effectively.

There are no short cuts to avoid the wilderness,

no alternative to apprenticeship.

A glimmer of this was commencing.

'Monkey'

At this time the ABC was showing "Monkey" on an early evening slot. Monkey is an allegorical tale of the monkey god who is tamed to the service of a holy Buddhist priest travelling to India to return with important scriptures.

'Monkey' together with 'Pigsy', the pig spirit, and the fish god 'Sandy', represent most of the self-orientation, greed, and arrogance that might be experienced by humankind, together with a camaraderie and a genuine loyalty to their priest Tripitaka. (This name is roughly equivalent to calling a story protagonist 'Bible' or 'Gita' in English) It is a Buddhist Pilgrim's Progress, but with warmth and fun.

Monkey is tamed by a gold band around his head, and sometimes by the interventions of the Buddha in female form.

After he had been highly inappropriate with some peach trees in Heaven, among other things, he tried to escape.

Then in coming up against 'The Pillars at the End of the Universe" he is confronted with them being the fingers of the Buddha's hand.

It is against this background that I am struggling with koan.

I am also looking at 'Monkey' with a new vision. And my experience of Donald Winnicott's teaching method was of more value than I had realised.

KOAN

I started on two koan:

'The bull jumped through the window and was caught by his tail.' was one.

The other was:
'A man put a gosling into a large glass jar with a narrow neck, fed it and cared for it, until it grew so large it could not get out'. How did the man get it out without killing it or breaking the glass?'

A military man is reputed to have put this to the master Nansen (Nan-Ch'uan, 748-835AD) who replied "Oh, Officer?" to which the officer responded in a dependent questioning manner, to which Nansen exclaimed (in the sense that we might use 'Voila!' even in English) "There! The goose is out!"

These two koan were my beginnings. My ignorance/arrogance in having two is comparable to that of Monkey.

I was drawn to them; they caught at my curiosity; they took a life in me in the sense that I worked on them, not only when I concentrated on them during zazen, but they assumed the power that the unsolved can assume if not cut off.

For all this, *'The goose is out'* had taken precedence over the other and became 'the koan'.

The Sydney Sun used to have a ten-letter word puzzle, which included finding as many words as possible from the ten letters, including the ten-letter word itself. I have been known to wake suddenly from an apparent deep sleep, suddenly knowing the solution.

Yet I am not suggesting that the knowing of a koan will generally come that way: sometimes it creeps upon you, you suspect a meaning and you really know it, but the truth of it and the implications of it, as well as the beliefs you must give up or reorganise to live with it, are so extensive, that a "Eureka!" would be inappropriate.

On the other hand, there may be the experience of sudden sight that changes the view of everything - this is called *kensho*.

> *I must add too, that at the back of this, I was always aware of 'the sound of one hand clapping'. After reading about it some years earlier in a newspaper, I had an impression of it as a satirised cliché. This left me with misgivings and a negative attitude to the koan.*

Development III

'ENCOUNTER WITH A GOOSE'

The value of koan lies in this process of struggle and in 'becoming' the koan

An explanation of a koan in terms of its meaning or even its value as a teaching tool would rightly bring ridicule and be destructive to the opportunities of those to come, but on the other hand to give Zen the appearance of special secrecy or initiation, would provide misunderstanding and confusion it could well do without.

Koan are not a distinctive handshake, they provide Zen with vitality and are conductors of insight to short circuit the insulation of verbal logic and much distracting knowledge.

It is the effect of a koan, including the development which occurs, that is important.

Then to ask, "Where has the traveler arrived?" So when I present views as from the next station up the line, without the scene from the train window in detail, it is to avoid depriving others of their own first-hand experience of the journey, and to avoid leaving them only with billboards that might seem obscene graffiti, obscure the beauty and obstruct the view.

It is said, however, that koan are there to help you avoid the high-falutin', and see what is in the middle of your face, what is around you and has been there from the beginning.

I had thought for a long time that if I were recommending a first koan to anybody, I would not start with these two. I thought *'The goose is out'* would be easier if there were others first. It is also one helped by a great deal of zazen practice and not helped by only having a little zazen practice.

Yet looking back I am glad that *'The goose is out'* was chosen first, but without training in the teaching of Zen, it is impossible to estimate the relative values of various koan for novices. Perhaps 'the one hand would be best?

I say this because knowing about the one hand, and yet deciding to work on others, was, as it happened, a way of letting the one hand in.

I don't know all my processes, but accept that the one hand might have been worked on somewhere among them.

Yet, having decided to apply effort and concentration, I didn't think I'd applied the to the one hand.

I followed *'the goose is out'* down many apparently unproductive side-alleys.

Development III

I was aware that the tone of voice, the question marks and other non-verbals, would have been part of the original exchange.

I thought that it must have already been used for teaching when the exchange with Nansen occurred. I used all sorts of logical approaches: the goose was living, it wasn't a closed system — it was at least fed: things were getting fouled up with goose droppings and so was my thinking. Why did Nansen say "Oh Officer?", and how did that translate from the Japanese and originally from the Chinese? How did he say it too?

Development III

'A COW CALLING FAINTLY'

sitting.

hands steadied first
breathe to the area just below the navel
eyes still

image of the dark mirror within
all quickly goes
to this
the breath is steady
      is quiet
the mirror is gone   there is wall before
plain wall
there is wall   sounds
a cow calling faintly
not one of our cows
there is wall

alertness
some aching in right shoulder
there is wall   breathing
becoming the breathing
is movement   now   breathing
air is needed - there is breathing
is wall   is
"Moo-oo."

In the stillness   the experience of 'Now' becomes very sharp
    it has been like this now for many months   the sounds
the space bar of the old Remington happens to my brain   it is as if the
awareness is contracted to what is right now   the film of experience
is finer   even the word 'now', with its 'n' sound first followed by
the strange vowel noise is too long verbal stuff   will not distract

No wonder they use zen for sword fighting, you could lose your head while
'verbal brain' is half through a word — let alone an idea

the neighbour's cow again   an image of the runty black and white
'cross-breads' on the darkened hill   they have been hungry
out there in the night   even though I can't see the cow
    and don't know her individually   they are there
all this represented in my central nervous system
  the goose isn't deaf or blind luckily she doesn't form lots of distracting
    static in her head

Development III

here is the wall and some aching muscles
the house creaks
the world is going on with its thing
and is registering in there
in where registering?
all of it
marvelous
but it isn't in there
my muscle can complain to my brain
it's not in there
it is where it is

wall
breathing
more breathing
more wall
no wind tonight
garment
at the wrist
sensation is distinct
it was there all the time
nowness very fine
as if one of those wool touch feelings
is happening one after another
spontaneous
quick images
couldn't really show what was happening in words
an illusion in the head?
spontaneously strike the wall with knuckle of the middle finger of the right hand

utterly predictable
including the pain
"What bullshit!" (the illusion)
the wall is a wall
it all processes
'outside' and inside' is the illusion

But it is what nets of nerve cells are doing!

the cow next door
even my aching muscle
isn't in my head;
its in my shoulder   the world

Development III

the moons of Jupiter are there
because there is an image
they are only there
        inside and outside
        all register in there
        all of it

the goose isn't silly enough
to think the man who feeds it
is in its head
but a process goes on
moves with spacetime
a changing occurs
this here   a changing
sets up a process
        all processed

its when you shut it up and leave
 only the hardware ticking over
with the software doing 'inhibit, inhibit'
that you know how big it is
it anticipates the future
moderates feelings
bring what it wants of the past
to be examined
but it does it as a whole
the overall picture
smell sound
finger

experience
in a landscape
picture to picture
see it without a theory
if you want air
you breathe   in and out
relaxing the hands
destroy the mirror
quietly   gone

> *Recreating early meditation with the irritability, tension, curiosity of unanswered questions will give a distorted view of zazen and the simplicity/prajna/mu that is zazen quality.*
>
> *This perspective is required because that was the issue and the development in 1980. But there is a respect for this tension that still survives; it is important to make sense of zazen experience, not to remain in a mode where 'the mind' becomes 'peaceful' and 'pure' and the will of 'I' unmodified.*
>
> *It would be too easy to do this more frequently and for longer at a time.*

I'm not left with a sense of the void or the unreality of the world: breathing is for air, the wall is hard: it is true that it all must be represented in my nervous system, and the processes of brain make order of it, even the supposed past and an attempt at the future, all 'now', but the brain and the world are working together.

> *For however marvelous the brain is, it is part of 'the everything'. It is not the 'brain' and the 'everything else'.*

Yet what is seen, even if illusion, if irrational — that is what is there: — a process in a brain.

Hollywood has foam rubber rocks that trick you when you are unable to examine them. The bill of a platypus feels rubbery: it looks hard like the bill of a duck. And there are many platypuses.

Our species is curious and tests it out personally. Skeptical too. So air is necessary and walls are hard, and it is when you hit the wall: wall and hand, pain, dust falls off the wall: the monk Wen-yên (later to become the influential master Ummon [d. 996 AD]) was not enlightened the times the gate did not crush his leg.

Such times did not teach him participation in 'the illusion'.

The gate and the leg interacted: "Crunch!" The gate, leg, pain is all then Mind — processes of wood and nerve and bone, but inconceivably united and consistent.

Development III

Yet an image can be experienced by having part of the cerebral cortex stimulated artificially during neuro-surgery without a general anaesthetic, arise in a dream or be distorted by drugs.

Thinking processes can generally test out what is around them, or have access to the testing of others to know if the reliable is indeed so. The most stringent method of testing the reliability of representations: is 'scientific method'.

But if the world and the processor are a single system, everything is as it is.

> Instead of using the drench-gun, I bought some molasses blocks which contained worm medicine. The cattle were supposed to lick it: I never saw them interested, and it lasted for years.
>
> During that winter as I threw the leaves of hay from the shed enclosure, I threw some well back from the far end, and, eventually, 'The Runner' would come up and eat while I hand fed Fernanda at the other end.
>
> During the following year I noticed that 'The Runner' had flies coming to her left eye, and that they were irritating her severely. I tried to get a look, but she wouldn't come close enough. The field glasses showed that it was a crusty patch on her lower eyelid. Her eye itself appeared normal.
>
>> Unfortunately, the white patches of a Hereford's skin,
>> particularly at the eye margin, are subject to a form of
>> cancer due to solar radiation called epithelioma.
>
> For some days I watched her from a distance, and could see it was becoming worse. I was also more certain that it was epithelioma.
> She had to be caught.
>
> I fed the cattle in the round-up yard with sweet lucerne hay for many days. After nearly a week 'The Runner' entered while I was well away and down-wind. 'The Little One' entered too — ate a few mouthfuls and came out. I let this happen for a few days.
>
> Then one day I walked back to the gate to pull it closed while 'The Runner' was in the little yard. The rotten rails were replaced by 'four-b'-three' and young iron bark.
>
> As the big gate (which opened into the yard), began to close, she saw it all. I was in the middle of the narrowing space. Without hesitation — she charged me... I jumped aside. She was free.

I was amazed: left standing there with mouth open: a new respect for became clear that 'The Runner's' eye was becoming worse and that she was suffering distress. This is not an easy cancer to treat, even in humans, where the freezing or radiation techniques cannot be used right against the eyeball She could not go on living with a growing cancer.
Catching her now would be very difficult.

They all fed in the little yard. Gertie and Fernanda scoffed most of the hay. Eventually 'The Runner' came back in to join them. I'd arranged for the carter's truck to come at a particular time, so she would not be penned unnecessarily.

I tied a long string to the cattle-yard gate. I took it across the creek through the fence of the main paddock and into a stand of melaleucas and spotted gum. I waited.

This time, when she eventually went in to the hay, I drew the gate slowly and surely closed. She ran to it when it clanged. I was worried she would injure herself, but she stayed against the far side shivering.

She must have been severely mistreated some time, although I often wondered if it was that she was bright enough to understand the dominance of man and dog, and her predicament as a preyed upon species. Her cancer was over a centimetre wide and ulcerated and growing under its crusty edges.

Certainly, Herefords were not bred for Australia and Latitude 33 deg. S, but rather for Latitude 53 deg. N.

'The Little One' stood off about twenty metres; she always finished up with some hay even when she didn't go in.

'The Runner' had the indignity of having a tail-tag put on and she went up the ramp into the truck, the driver shouting "Hoy! Hoy!" at her. I remembered as an adolescent taking a very ill cat called Mrs Glamour to the council yard to be gassed. It came back to me as if it happened only yesterday.

These gentle animals had their own character, their social life and their problems. I saw my own ignorance and insensitivity in this mirror.

Development III

a clear afternoon
at burning time
the family works in gum smoke

'THE SOLES OF MY SHOES?'

The goose is about 'boundaries': mine and yours.

Here 'The Muddle-headed Wombat' comes to my aid. He looks for a zipper to take off his skin. And Winnicott and Erikson teaching about play: children's processes are outside in their game, on display to anybody who will stop and watch.

Again, the student argument, where are the boundaries of 'you' and 'I': the sole of my shoes, the bony case of my skull, the pia mater? Supposing there is a something that is apart from everything else, we are having some trouble with separating it from everything else.

The goose's apparent problem is immediately obvious: it is a glass jar that everybody can see and bang their knuckle against. So why does this military man ask Nansen such a question? Does he think Nansen is a slight-of-hand expert, a magician?

Again Wen yen's leg: caught in the gate and severely injured. The gate, the pain, the injury — better a touch from the master's staff to know that unity.

The goose has her glass jar; you have your skin. And through that skin? Light and contact and waves in the air, chemicals to nasal receptors, hands make print, the blind man sings and the deaf woman's face and hands tell a romantic saga.

Yet the processor is within that skin; it is of the same order as everything, even if of a different order of complexity.

How does the tree think? How does the table think?
Monkey was still in The Buddha's hand; the bull had his difficulties with the window, but he wasn't caught by his horns or his head, but by his tail.

THE AIR I BREATHE

I was driving along in the G.M. Commodore months later when it really came to me. I had been aware that the habits of zazen were coming into my thinking at other times when I wasn't formally practicing. I'd found it altered my attitude and the sharpness of my response in other situations too.

What came was a feeling of wonder, of unity with the world, and it was a unity in which I was not locked up in my skin.

I was the bunch of jacaranda leaves, the bridge parapet, the birds.

The sense was so strong that during a flight in a small plane in fairly rough weather, I was the wind and wingtips, the seat, the plane, the clouds, the down-drafts, and I wanted to retreat to the cabin and then my skull, but I could not, because all that was registering was all that was registering — the definition of boundary was a convention.

I realised that the Australian aboriginal people had been saying this consistently: the unity of people and land: it is not only the man's trees, the woman's house, the child's swinging branch; everybody knows it; it was there all the time. Everything is in its place.

From where I could now see it, this was obvious, but I wondered if it would have been possible without all the consideration of 'Boundary' issues I'd been exposed to in my earlier training.

But my culture had fostered my belief that there was a 'something' bounded by my skin or my clothes or my skull or by the limits of my neurones, that was me, and that everything else was other — object. The language is structured that way. "I see the orange tree", I say, as I look up.

From another viewpoint, some of the light from the orange tree is passing through my cornea and is registered, perceived, integrated with my experience of the orange tree. In contrast my zazen experience allows me to experience virtually all orange tree, so that 'Now' is 'orange tree'.

An outside observer would see me, fingers still lightly on the keyboard, looking out the window; he reads the screen and he has some idea of what is happening.

He knows all my experiences are a process proceeding from one nanosecond to the next; the orange tree experience is part of a unified experience of the everything happening in a nervous system.

He sees me and the orange tree doing our thing and he is part of it too.

I've been writing Development Three in this subject/object form because that is the conventional use of English language, and, will be most comfortable for readers in gauging this part of my experience.

I accept that my skin is there, but what is being processed in my nervous system has only an arbitrary division at 'skin'. It may be that it is represented by a continuous process of depolarised membranes triggering further depolarisation, but it is reliable. The orange blossom has a reliable effect. If it was July, I might pick an orange and eat it.

Each nervous system might similarly process, and, as such, be any variety, quality, multiplicity, combination of The Everything, including what is being communicated to him or her. But I, and all that out there, back there, anticipated there, registered by my nervous system, it is all myself.

And there is nothing apart from myself.

That came suddenly while looking at wall; all of it represented in there (including the wall): all of it is myself; if I read a book an aspect of it becomes myself: — and there isn't anything else.

What we need here is a cartoon of the observer going away from my rooms, saying to his spouse, "He actually thinks he's an orange tree. Where does that leave me?"

Was he serious about the question, where might he go?

Development III

THE RIDGE POLE?

While I had undergone a sudden and satisfying experience of comprehension over 'The goose is out', it was not the experience Suzuki was describing.

I was drawn to the Buddha's principal question of 'I ness', the existence of an 'I' in the works, a 'ridge-pole in the house' in his metaphor. What had I done with that?

My thinking about it was only that: thinking — a wordy weighing of the evidence.

The Evidence:

On one side the case for 'I', 'the ridge pole':

a. The convention of subject and object built into the language,

b. naming as 'I' some of the knowledge processes experienced.

c. the philosophers — some directly, some by implication,

d. the requirement to identify and give a name to a particular individual body,

e. and one's life long conviction about being an 'I'.

On the other side there was my awareness how a strong and adequate self functioned with good integration of perception, intuition, sensation, thinking and feeling ... Now.

An overall process of other pivotal processes.

Essentially it is the same 'five skandas' which Shakyamuni saw had no substance.

This healthy combination of processes is equivalent to 'true self'.

It was also what I had learnt and experienced about 'self' from early understanding of Rogers. This interest is a reflection of psychotherapeutic thinking since the Mid-seventies about how a child's 'self' develops with adequate adult empathy.

The issue for the psychotherapy of people with personality disorder (disorders of 'self') is the treatment of painful and handicapping 'I' demands which lead to troubled relationships.

Therapy requires an alliance where the feelings are recognised and contained, the 'I' centred elaborations left behind, and the immediate processes of a healthy self valued as they are reflected by the therapist.

'The self' as synthesised capable process, moves in contrast to 'I' — the latter a series of beliefs — essentially firm memories of mental process, bulletin boards which tend to close off after coming to conclusions.

Some of these make claims on processes of the self, particularly to expend energy on maintaining the shaky 'I' image. And when this 'I image' is indispensable and desperately maintained because it is confused with the processes of self, it presages distress and unhappiness.

This is at the core of psychotherapy and the core of Buddhism.

The self (as proces.0s) on the other hand, is totally open to interaction with the available processes of The Universe. And this is so whether they are within or without the skin. While this capacity might be called 'the self', to slip into calling even the most capable self a something/somebody is too easy.

It is too easy to see the packaging and be interested in 'I'bulletin boards, too easy to be distracted from the organism's nature requiring its processes to be one with its environment.

The Buddhist issue is whether both 'self' and 'I' beliefs are valid. 'I' and 'the other', subject and object: beliefs, a viewpoint from an arbitrarily separate body, arrived at by 'the self' — in error?

Implications? The self in this construction is complicated process.

And 'I' amounts to reprocessed constructions of a second order. Neither suggest any 'something' indicative of a permanent 'I'.

How does anybody adapt to such a view?

One implication is first in importance:

When the division between the 'other' and 'I' is meaningless, and other famous divisions: Heaven and Earth, body and soul, have lost their hold, the sense of basic 'oneness' of everything gathers itself to the point where active denial would be required to shut it out.

The bull loses interest in the window; he watches David Suzuki on the tele.

DEVELOPMENT IV

Bewildered goose

The issue of 'I'ness' came from a direction other than the awareness of 'no-boundary'.

The Western view of individuality was ingrained: a view of detailed individuality with a distinct boundary between 'me' and 'other'. Now I was looking at it again.

And it was day-to-day living that mattered. There seemed to be so many implications. It was confusing: is the other person part of self too? Does the boundary stop there?

That was not easy, despite my having written articles about looking at multi-person systems when making assessments of families.

Which was the best system in which to intervene? The marriage? Parent and child? Child on their own? This led to advocating therapy involving twosomes, families and greater families.

Yet there was no going back to see the boundaries in the old way: the focus on skin and individual brain was overshadowed as the implications of oneness grew.

I was struck by the awareness of breath being a continual exchange with outside. The photons entering my eye had only left the sun some minutes previously, and my sense of the sun's heat and the weight of the shopping bag was all about the complex exchanges of body and environs.

I think my difficulties were because I half knew the Buddha's central issue about 'I'ness'. I questioned too the thesis that suffering was due to 'wanting', and most relieved when desires were put aside.

Earlier, I'd been strongly influenced by Karen Horney's view on unhappiness/neurosis being a direct result of the formation of an ideal-self that was impossible, or was forced to exist in personal belief, despite great reality contradictions.

The unhappiness arose because there was a wish to be that ideal self in a great magic leap, and rage occurred at the appearance of evidence that it was not so.

Later I was helped in understanding the pain of such people's defenses by the work of Masterson and Kohut.

I was also aware of the hurt and struggle so many have with envy, a malignant form of craving from earliest life. Not only is there craving, but destructive focus on others for apparently having that which is craved.

I was testing out the whole Buddhist thesis against what I already knew. I was aware that wanting to eat the meal already on the table was not the point, but the danger was wanting excessive control and predictability.

On the other hand, where there is a sense of helplessness and unpredictability, the organism is highly stressed. Yet the more control desired, the more vulnerable to suffering the man, woman, family or nation becomes.

However, not to imagine, not believe possible, not to dare, is neither adaptive nor simple human such- ness. Nevertheless, as dilemmas such as these arise, there is a middle way to be seen.

Yet, here was I, growing oranges on my branches — in the sun.

> *During the two odd years of the struggle recounted in Development 1V, the 'no boundaries' awareness is used to test the validity of the basis of Buddhism, first of its tenets and then of its critics — issue by issue — necessarily mindful of personal ignorance and disorganised awareness.*
>
> *Some aspects are not accepted, some accepted as mythic allegory, and others as only partly understood. The struggle to see the essential from the background continues, until it clears somewhat in Norwegian twilight.*

Residues of ignorance

The dharma it is called in Buddhism: the teaching — the law: what a Buddhist hopes to know, understand or 'see'.

Now, half knowing, but without any unification to what I knew: bounaries, leaves and sunshine — suffering? This added to my reservations. Suspicions lurked in my thinking throughout this time. Recreating this is important, because it represented major disquietude about Buddhism that came from varied sources.

It was more than skepticism. At one level was the suspicion that the well-known defense mechanism of the 'I', called 'reaction-formation' was being used or even being recommended. I'd seen the destructiveness of that so many times:

Briefly, when some people have hostile feelings, these might cause so much guilt or impugn the self-image, that emotional energy is channeled to sentiments and driven behaviour of the opposite nature.

If rage were really converted to love that would be fine.

But 'reaction formation' (a reaction against the true feeling) contains elements of the feeling/attitude being converted: the parent who is caring for their child while defending in this way against rejection and rage is most vulnerable. Yet they work hard for the child: great meals, clean clothes, expressions of loving sentiment; but it is done from a distance and the heart must be obscured.

It does not allow intimacy as does the spontaneous article. Adults might not notice it: children know the difference.

Any true transformation of emotional energy must necessarily come from facing the feelings ... and suffering through their centre.

To do this with some awareness of one's true nature is much easier.

Also the context and perspective, the position from which I viewed day to day happenings had certainly changed, and my perception, feelings, were different to those I would have had previously. It is difficult to be as angry at those beside you on 'The wheel of life', when you and they are changing as one.

Development IV

THE WHEEL OF LIFE

What of *samsara*, 'The wheel of life, death and rebirth' — rebirth according to merit?

An ancient metaphor: creatures living, breeding and dying, fecundity and decay: the wheel turns — moves inexorably, those on it subject to time and loss, frustration and suffering.

'The Wheel' implies the extended 'cause-and-effect' of the Vedic belief - the consequences of merit or evil behaviour would follow into a new life.

I was aware of the Buddhist impact on this belief: because in Buddhism any person could find freedom from this karmic destiny by being enlightened.

Buddhism immediately stepped beyond caste. Shakyamuni took action to prevent suffering from the pain of 'The wheel of life; indeed, from the belief itself?

Later in India, when much of Buddhist wisdom was internalised again by the Hindu religion, this pivotal aspect of dharma was lost. The inertia of privilege and tradition continued the justification of the false beliefs associated with caste. If it were not for this factor the Hindu and Buddhist religions would have extensive common ground.

In thinking about the validity of 'The wheel of life', I could see here that 'the oneness' went on and on, that if 'I' was a delusion, the oneness would bring rebirth without knowledge of identity-specifics, and, in those terms, rebirth was inevitable.

But the notion of an 'I' being reborn as a more developed being without the 'I' from the previous life (as a reward for merit, or as an aspect of development of an individual soul), and this is what traditional karma implied, was contradictory to the main thesis.

This view of karma seemed contradiction, confusion and distress — not credible. At this stage, while such a reaction left a muddled and unsatisfactory view, it was appropriate. However, quiet experienced sitting would have seen the many evolvements of 'The always so'.

I can remember wondering humorously whether some of the six segments of 'The wheel of life' would correspond to being an organism on a planet in another solar system, perhaps in one of the numerous other galaxies.

The context of Shakyamuni's time was that the religions of India reflected a general belief in rebirth through many thousands of existences. Despite the gods of the Aryan invaders, including Brahma the supreme deity, this rebirth to further suffering as animal, insect, or bird, was basic in the people's beliefs. Shakyamuni would save them from this, as well as the caste system, and the total dominance by the Brahman priests brought South by the Aryans.

But if 'I' is illusory, and the rest process, the primitive view of rebirth is negated.

Yet 'The wheel of life' with its Heaven (gods), fighting Titans, (demigods), human earth, world of animals, Hell (demons) and domain of hungry ghosts, is a formalised version of the peoples' beliefs, and is put up with the clear indication that escape from it is possible: I first approached it as a question about the difference between being reborn as another organism after one's death, or being reborn as a contemporary.

As I lift my garage door in the morning, the skink who lives between the bottom of the door and the concrete hurries out, and I am careful to keep my feet still until he's under cover. The garage-door, the skink, the concrete, the hand that lifts the door: all of the oneness.

Mind you, there are bulls who would jump through the window, and some who think they have, but haven't realised what has happened to their tail. A skink wouldn't be caught by his tail, as he is able to drop it and go on. But a skink would never dream of jumping through a window.

Yet being a biologist in the year 2260 is 'pie in the sky': At least I am a skink. So went the struggle with 'I', still caught in the ignorance of 'something/then'.

Development IV

"May 'The Force' be with you."

I had heard of Zen having a dubious image, associated with quick mannerisms and superiority.

Respected friends have had poor experiences of one-upmanship, detachment and indifference in the name of 'Zen'.

From my own observations, zazen could be used in countless ways.

I remember thinking that George Lucas' Star Wars films had a pseudo-philosophy in fairy-tale form of 'The Force', to be translated as 'God' by some, and magic power by others.

The association of it with telekinesis: lifting space ships, strangling a victim from a distance: put it in the realm of omnipotent magic. If it was not for that, there were many elements in it of the personal strengths realised from the practice of zazen.

Lucas said strengths could be used for good or evil — for that read: in the service of "The Everything", or in the service of a greedy 'I'. It is easy to imagine enhanced perception and freedom from illusion, used both ways.

There is too, the ill-informed and stereotyped view of Japanese culture that would equate zen with strong and ruthless group behaviour, used in the service of parochial interests. In contrast, history indicates that Buddhism, and Zen in particular, has been among the balancing factors to counteract such influences in Japanese culture.

Nevertheless, I would concede that sitting without wisdom and development, could bring about some of the problems faced when Dr Frankenstein's monster was animated.

And later came the view, that adept sitting with a good appreciation of 'just this' brings responsibility to see through the small gate that is not there — and see 'humility'.

"Zazen — nothing in it?"

My progress with zazen requires attention.

My skepticism whether there was anything in it, was changed to an awareness that there was more to it than I could readily conceive. I had approached zazen at one level as an opportunity to observe my mind functioning, particularly while bringing about some experimental states of mind as if this would help me know the nature of myself.

I thought I could do this just as an observer of any other phenomenon. While this approach was misleading and now seems intellectual foolishness, it at least got me started.

But there was now much more. It was a sense of intimacy which was with my socks, the air entering my body, the clouds and the light. I could understand how a painter might be driven to share such experience. I was noticing that when the inner commentary was stilled, and the past or future was kept away — unless they came as immediate intuitive knowing, I was experiencing a quality that was an authentic appreciation of 'no boundary'.

It changed everyday life. I was listening and observing more acutely — my receiving apparatus, already trained, became even more efficient, and that together with my not having the illusion of hiding in my skin:

Here was the happening, the awareness so much sharper.

So often what was required was not speech or even action, but more observation and understanding, a reaching out to show my fellows they were received, their hurt and perplexity shared, and I would stay with it.

Sometimes there was the illusion that events were happening very slowly. In practice, zazen has a powerful effect on subjective time.

During what I thought of as a mental Spring-clean, the mirror that is not there, the breathing, the line of sight, and the birds stage-left: even they are not in attention — time is as if suspended.

However, when an issue of mindfulness is introduced, and concentration allows of the single issue without unnecessary detail, much time might pass on the clock without seeming to do so.

Certainly, I was aware that time was necessary to create 'I'. By 'time' I mean having a thick film of 'now' (Say, at least 600 milliseconds).

But the most simple and direct experience is that the practice of zazen itself obliterates 'I'.

Holding the mind without any quasi-verbal conclusions or ruminations without memories or speculations — 'not I' exists.

This allows 'I', then 'I' makes its own illusion of subjective time.

To paraphrase 'The Diamond Sutra': 'I' is the name given to some products of the self, but there is no such thing as an 'I' (or indeed, a self: there is process dealing with virtual representations, active codings in a nervous system), therefore it is called 'I'.

THE ONE BRIGHT PEARL

As in 'Special Relativity', spacetime is when/where matter/energy is, so time and its apparent flow is when/where you are: experiencing changes in your nervous system. There is no division or discontinuity.

If an experiment was to be devised to test such breaks in Oneness they would look like a magic show such as you would see at the Circus or some other Late Twentieth Century version of vaudeville.

The magician is assisted by a glamourous young woman, who disappears from her cabinet only to reappear later somewhere else, or even return after disappearing. The audience knows they are bound to continuity in time and place, that her body has travelled through a lifetime without a distortion of the unity of time or place.

They are all enlightened about utter Oneness in all four dimensions. They know the magician is demonstrating the impossible. That is why it is so exciting.

Eihei Dogen (1200 - 1253), Zen master of Thirteenth Century Japan, who was pivotal in bringing Zen from China to Japan, expressed this notion clearly. "All the Universe is 'One bright pearl'"

ITS APPARENT FORM

My perception from my koan tells me it is 'all represented actively in there': — the nervous system; yet everything is in its place; object and subject is an arbitrary division as the whole does its matter/energy/spacetime gavotte.

Physics is fully aware of complementarity: the observer measures the result, determines the result (is the result), — even if the wave/particle might have been registered as a wave after passing through a diffraction grating but on the other hand might have been registered as a particle on the photographic plate.

And the excitation state/pattern of the neural net is the ultimate photographic plate where Reality replaces reality. All this means is that the colour and shape, the pitch and timbre are processes of the neural net that give The Sum of Processes its apparent form, and this must function well enough for the world to appear as it does.

I have known many who come at this issue from altering consciousness with drugs. It is not usual for them to put what they learn from perceptual aberration together with what is learned from other methods, such as meditation or natural illusion — then — see the implications, take this point of development and move on.

Neither positive nor negative

Then there is also the image that Buddhism seeks negation, believes in nothingness, passivity and withdrawal from the world.

I can remember thinking when I first read Christmas Humphries as a nineteen- year-old, that the monk pursuing a life of meditation with the aim of himself finding nirvana was both unadaptive and uninspiring. Sadly, Teilhard, even in his later life, did not know Buddhism enough to have gone past this view. Indeed he dismissed it on shallow acquaintance.

But Thomas Merton, Cistercian monk, author, scholar of the Christian dharma became closely involved with understanding Zen. He was clear in affirming its spiritual validity, and was aware of how it could be like Christianity if only 'faith' was added.

At this stage I read the contemporary Swiss Catholic priest, Hans Küng: theologian, teacher at Tübingen in Germany, whose rights to teach as a Catholic Theologian had already been withdrawn by the Congregation for the Doctrine of Faith. He is publishing in his lifetime, and not sequestered from interaction with the world, as happened to Teilhard.

I found him highly readable and the breadth of his knowledge of religion and philosophy fascinating.

Küng had struggled to understand Buddhism and certainly knew more about it than I, but early indicated that there were almost insurmountable difficulties in understanding it.

In his own way he struggled with 'Mu' and saw "negation of negation" as the apex of this way. He wonders aloud if tradition is responsible for the affirmation behind the double negative.

Like Merton, he does not stop as if at an impasse of apparent nihilism in the words used to describe Buddhist development, he tries to go further.

I continue to be haunted by the difficulty of not knowing Kung's intuition and gestalt functioning. I wonder if there is but little difference in what he is saying but he too, is handicapped by knowledge and words.

This leads to the issue that if 'I' is not, what is there? What quality has it? If realising 'not I' is a goal in itself, is this the important truth, and so, how does 'seeing' from this viewpoint compare with the illusion?

> *Still to come was the total sense of minuteness - only process, aware of a smidgin of itself.*

Development IV

'SUNYATTA'

Some difficulties with misunderstanding of Buddhism have been in the translation of the Sanskrit sunyatta. In China this was translated to the Chinese equivalent of 'void', and in English is translated as 'nothing' or 'emptiness'. All of these terms are implicitly negative.

'Void' in Chinese belief at the time was a formless something that pervaded everything rather like the 'ether' of the Nineteenth century scientists.

Sunyatta however has a highly positive connotation, indicating a special state of mind free from the static of compulsive thought, awake, alert, aware of everything as it is in 'the now'. And as such is equivalent to Mind (the experienced process), and dhyana / meditation, but it is truly negative in the sense of being no 'thing'.

Zazen experience and knowing the phenomena of very deep sleep, called delta sleep, gradually gave an awareness of a different nature, the importance of which was not realised. Even the movement of mind process arises from utter nothing, from unorganised movement, from the great 'not-conscious'.

The 'not-conscious' was at the back of every action, blended with every thought. It is as if the reaction in the flame, all heat and change, ignores the captive flux that is 'candle'. Similarly, looking at the bay: it is choppy one day — the waves breaking on the jetty — the next day it is calm. Truly 'being' and 'not being' are of one essence.

Initially I was sustained by my habit of pushing myself at the truth whatever the pain, and my gradual appreciation of this new view of the world. I was sustained by Shakyamuni himself; the identification with his first crisis went deeply; the compassion of his caring was unquestionable.

Another factor that helped greatly with the dilemmas of half-knowing was the little book by Irmgard Schloegl recommended in the Introduction. It was implicit with feeling and confidence. The zen she exemplified gave a sense of inherent morality. The heart it spoke of behind development, was a heart that would grow, persist in a world where the complications of social existence were unavoidable

"... AS THE VEIN OF GOLD GOES"

Caught: realising I only had some of it. It was most unsatisfactory. Confusion, uncertainty, and a sense that there was always the danger of closing my mind after taking a conclusion too quickly.

I feel for those stuck there, particularly if they are tempted to stay with some of their knowledge and not to see it in the perspective of what might yet develop.

Note that my understanding is accompanied by 'logical stuff'. I was somewhat like a miner, tunnelling and tunnelling as the vein of gold goes, but stopping to find strong timbers to support the roof. I was to be helped in going forward by knowing that science itself was confronting at its boundaries a conflict with logic, not only with the uncertainty principle, but the whole issue of complementarity.

Newton's predictable Universe, the wound-up clock, was a lost image as 'quantum mechanics' was born. Predestination broke up in a sea of 'uncertainty'.

Also, I was testing out the view of oneness against the philosophers, but knew that Buddhism could not be described in simple philosophic terms.

I had recognition that the oneness — 'everything', was as is represented in a nervous system, but also that everything is as it is, and can be tested — tested in a highly systematic manner — scientific method — another process. Later I would say "It moves as it moves", but could not see the difference then. "Does as it does", is another version.

Science would have previously abided with a contrived objectivity, and rightly so as this avoided the mistakes of wishful thinking, guessing and attention seeking.

Now there is a realisation in the philosophy of science that perception/knowledge is specifically subjective, yet if it remains consistent and agreed upon by the subjectivity of many, then it may temporarily be considered valid and reliable.

But the zen approach is necessarily without 'the objectivity illusion', even while recognising the value of striving for it. However it is only subjective in the special sense of 'Oneness', where 'subjective' and 'objective' are meaningless.

Development IV

"... AND NOTHING ELSE"

Both zazen and *The goose is out* left me with a number of givens: the subject/object unity, the awareness of a unity that is called Mind (a process of fluid virtual representations) and nothing else. Mind could test things as they are, and bring about growth. Mind could be stilled and itself demonstrate aspects of 'suchness'.

I knew there was more and that I had pieces of it: I had some special knowledge but no real general knowledge, but what I had was so strong the rest must be there. And it wasn't hiding.

On the other hand I knew all this intellectual working out would fall away in day to day living. Such intellectual formulations are of little value in shaping living.

Work was such a personal process, and being tired seemed to be a way of life. I fell into the habits of 'I'. My sense of subject/object unity would diminish. I would fall back to 'self against the world.' While not finding the understanding I knew was there, it seemed difficult to hold what I did understand in a workaday life where the expectations were according to my old habits.

I told myself some was due to my omnipotence in even trying to understand outside the sangha (essentially a Buddhist community). How would it be to live within a Buddhist culture? I suppose I would have grown up being iconoclastic about whatever type of Buddhism was practiced

'THE WAY'

The notion of dharma (Sanskrit), sometimes dhamma (Pali) came up again and again. I developed an intuitive sense of the meaning, although I realised it had translatable meanings referring to 'law', 'teaching', but the intuitive meaning was something like, the teaching of 'the way' of 'the everything', in the sense of both 'practice' and 'path', or particular qualities of 'the everything' as in 'virtue' and 'truth'.

I thought it was best rendered in English as "The 'suchness' of 'the always so', which said something beautiful that I didn't understand. But that beauty is in the essence of Buddhism.

In the origin of Buddhism, the pain of desire, sickness and dying, rebirth and more suffering, could be first relieved by dealing with desire and second by going outside samsara.

The Taoist could go with 'the way', bend with it, accept it, be happy by doing what was required effortlessly. Buddhism that concentrated on 'suffering' was poor quality to the Taoist.

However, the real comparison was that Buddhism could transcend samsara and take action for the suffering of many. However, they were essentially alike the two, except in transcendence and action.

Taoism has had so much influence on Zen Buddhism, that the first Patriarch of Ch'an Buddhism in Southern China (the blue-eyed monk Bodhidharma who came from India with 'the teaching outside scriptures' early in the Sixth Century AD) would quote the Tao te Ching.

My previous knowledge of the Tao te Ching was leading me to see many parallels between the Tao and the Dharma. But Zen as Buddhism has an activity and a development of itself that is in contrast to the Taoist life.

Development IV

Karma?

Karma was a word that I had understood as meaning 'fate', 'kismet', and I was aware that 'New Age' devotees, would use it to indicate an attachment between individuals sharing a common fate from incarnation to incarnation.

This implied acceptance of the belief in reincarnation of an individual soul, that 'Atman' would discard the body and be born again: to a higher caste, in Heaven, as a cockroach? Morally it implied that goodness would be rewarded and that wrong action not only brought pain and suffering to a new life, but would require reparation.

These beliefs were held across the Indian subcontinent, and, in the orthodox Buddhism of many countries, there is acceptance of cause-and-effect of a meritorious or unharmonious life bringing about a higher or lower position on The Wheel of Life with rebirth.

But who knows what this higher or lower position is: surely it depends on viewpoint?

If you look carefully at the life of the skink who lives under my garage door: well, he's actually lower than me, and he does become unsettled when I take his roof on high, but he looks very healthy, he doesn't have an 'I' problem, and he gets much energy directly from the sun.

There is an action of the world (of suchness) that needs be accepted. It can be referred to as karma, just as 'fate', looking at what is past, refers to an occurrence, and is seen as a real event; however, used here, its meaning might be misunderstood as a 'deserved fate' as it is traditionally used: although the in- evitable consequences of some form of behaviour may require its use implying simple causality.

When it is used in these pages however, it refers to good or bad outcome in the broadest sense, and with no implication of guilt and punishment, and not in a 'New Age' predestination sense, or indeed, in an orthodox Buddhist sense of elaborate "cause and effect' from one individual life to the next.

Used in its 'action of the world Now' sense, it is 'suchness' and may well be loving, fulfilling, kicking, painting ... whatever.

> *This explanation of karma as struggled with then, highlights the essence of Hinayana and Mahayana Buddhism. Hinayana lays the foundation: the awareness of impermanence and the struggles against it of each and every creature, which, as evolved life, must*

have wants, competition and insecurity by its very nature. The Hinayana view to escape the delusions, with self-sufficient moral unity, is the core of all Buddhism.

The Mahayana view is whole, seeing the full implications of every event interconnected, and the action of one quantum of humanity spreading to the karma of all, bringing good quality as light fills a room.

Development IV

PRACTICAL ZEN

Zen from its Chinese phase of development was immensely practical. One of the basic differences from earlier Buddhism is that Zen is rooted in the day-to- day world.

Zen is about preparing food, washing dishes, speaking kindly to others, and choosing a gentler way of relating.

But my zazen practice was not settled.

I had experimented with cushions, was able to get a foot to the opposite thigh, with much stretching, but it was quite untenable.

I watched Australian aborigines on video to observe their easy sitting.

I sometimes did zazen in this position, but it was still less distracting in a straight chair; and even better once I learnt to discipline my eyes wherever I was. The senses were not with the viewpointing.

At this time, I would say the important physical elements were the back in a straight but natural position, discipline over the hands and eyes, and privacy.

This time of half-understanding was helped by the goose. I could come back to it as a way to test experience, and the utter nowness during zazen became a creative field. Suzuki after *'The goose is out'* was like reading a completely new book.

The implications of the koan were to be faced and brought into line with life experience. Mind was everything. Yet Mind was no thing and there is no such thing as 'a mind'. And when tested by Mind the world was as it was: knuckles on wall.

There was a reliability that was tested by experiment, and would allow for abstractions (theories) that could explain and predict that reliability. Bread was bread, the mountains were mountains, this suchness might be Mind, but it was as it was (particularly when tested).

This type of thinking came as a corollary of the koan. It was as though there must be some path of Zen to which 'Science is' was a major kensho; not only was there a suchness to know, but it could be tested by experiment. All this amounts to, is that there is no requirement to be passive in knowing the suchness of the everything.

After *'The goose is out'*, the leaf, the cloud, are not other, and so much more interesting: the curiosity, fraternity with everything formerly seen as if 'there', is zest to 'the 'now' experience'. Even to have theories for the process of testing out observations, is to have two processes that are fine if not confused with each other.

And because 'Mind' actively interprets: even perception itself is interpretation: the testing and re-testing of science will always be necessary, as these without testing lead off on elaborate and confusing tangents. Judgement can then be distorted by an untested idea, or by a wish that arises to provide resolution for strong feelings.

But it is obvious at this stage that development is the senior partner to science. Although an essential method and viewpoint, science is not about Identity, Meaning and Ethic. Even when science finds a general theory of The Cosmos of great beauty and balance, it will be the interpretation made in Mind and the implications for the conduct of action which is Value.

Pulsars and Planets

What did my koan tell me about the dharma? Was it a name for my subject/object fusion? The no thing that becomes, changes in the infinitesimally tiny 'now'? Yet there is the 'teaching/law of the everything' view of dharma? Was the dharma referring to 'the enormous remnant' that I had found by looking at myself — the 'what was left' when 'I' was gone?

At that time, my interested was in pulsars. A pulsar's emissions in the radio spectrum are picked up by a radio-telescope like the one at Parkes; a pulsar is emitting radio waves, usually from another galaxy countless light years from Earth, and the evidence indicates pulsars are likely to be small but rapidly spinning neutron stars of great density.

This leads me to think about all that might be, or, might not be experienced.

But I cannot see what life on the planet Zlelt is like, but I could go to Easter Island if I wished. The planet Zlelt (I just thought of it writing the last sentence) can be given an imaginary life that I might spend years elaborating; whereas I already know something of Easter Island, but I haven't put my hand against the stone as I have with Vineland's statues at Oslo.

I know there are new aspects of The Everything as yet not experienced by this body's processes, and that The Everything as experienced changes. (I could go out to the Seville orange tree and within minutes find a member of an insect species I have never before observed.)

So, despite the 'all that there is now', there is the potential everything that might be registered in one nervous system, a 'once and future everything'. This was sure, because my 'no boundaries' was temporal as well as spatial, despite the impossibility of anticipating the myriad uncertainties of the unseen future. "A potential everything."

I decided I liked it. There was heart in it. Of it was this planet and its organisms, its Buddhas, its people loving and working, its flowers, mountains and seas, suffering, changes and loss.

But what of the hundred billion odd stars in this galaxy (and their planets), there is surely an absolute everything that can only be known from samples!?

"Stop! I am chopping it up — technical, tied up with logic". My zazen practice tells me the Mind I experience is all there is and there is nothing else.

But Everything changes, or, put another way: 'Mind' changes: 'Mind' is nothing but change and it has no boundaries. It is whole in all dimensions.

Shakyamuni spoke of unity with other Buddhas from other kalpas — enormous periods of time from his similes about mountains being worn down by the occasional brush of a wing — perhaps from one 'big bang' to the next?

The Anthropic Principle (our point of view must be from where and when our particular species is and according to how it processes) indicates that time is a view point from the position of 'matter who thinks'. 'And' in theory we can reduce it to trillionths of a nanosecond which makes it ridiculous - another illusion: it leaves us with changes, moves, dances....

Is the dance a unity? Of course, it is! I've been letting myself be confused by words again, as if the 'now' of physics or 'now' of everyday speech is 'Now' which I am coming to know from sitting.

'Now' is 'Mind' itself, but both words distract.

There are further things that are as they are, but cannot be known. How long it takes an undiscovered planet in orbit around a star in the Large Magellanic Cloud to complete one pass around its primary cannot be known by Mind (registered in this nervous system). On the other hand, Mind allows the possibility.

How to see from the valley the highest peak of them all? Size and complexity, simplicity and beauty: you sit firmly on your planet with a warm heart and straight back — accept the true however it comes.

Dogen's view that 'time' is 'still' and everything else is not.

IDENTITY

Where would this take me? I'm asking about identity — the "Who am I?" question.

Pirsig gave a clear account of his coming up against a powerful understanding/enlightenment that his pedestrian self later would only allow to be partly true, or partly important, but enlightenment was followed by a psychiatric-ward where he lost chunks of his identity — even his personality, as we saw reflected in his young son's perception of him.

How can identity changes be contained? And how valid are they?

I remember some twenty odd years ago, meeting a young man in his early twenties in the admission office of a large psychiatric hospital. My role was of admission-officer.

The young man was calm and relaxed. He had been persuaded to come for admission because he had become aware he was the Son of God, and he would say this truthfully and simply. He smiled with awareness of his predicament when he said he wanted people to be at peace and be good to one another. He said he was unwanted. He stayed for a couple of days, and said he wished to go back to his job, and that's what happened.

That was unusual; every month or so the Admission Ward receives a person who is excited, sometimes incoherent and has understood everything. They are often euphoric, and frequently identified with Jesus or his mother.

Some tell of receiving special understanding from God. They are frightened and distressed, usually by 'supernatural' phenomena, very angry at being in the Admission Ward, and shocked by their situation. Some are trapped within their narcissism.

Others attract serious diagnoses and treatment and get 'better'
in the same sense that Pirsig did by adapting with an acceptable enough role. But Pirsig was able to hold his experience that Mind, Quality, Now, Reality, The Buddha, were one and the same — and to write about it later.

Theorists say these people have lost their sense of personal boundary, and their identity was poorly formed and has broken up as it was vulnerable to do. They say the illness comes first in some instances, such as mania or an exacerbation of schizophrenia, and then the content of chaotic thought is partly an expression of personality and culture.

How many say "Eureka!" at the end of much effort, concentration and mindfulness, and would not be accepted as socially appropriate, or not accepted because they cannot keep their thought and / or behaviour within areas defined as sanity? They are expected to put timbers to the roof?

But the identity issue? Was it really an issue?
In response to the question, "Who are you?", does somebody who is aware they do not have a special boundary at their skin begin to panic because they should have one.

If one said one was part of a twosome, or a skink who lived under a garage door, or an orange tree: how would that be? Equally unacceptable might be the "What a silly question" response. Easier to tell the truth?

Development IV

Two American novels

Nirvana, is another word from Buddhism in the living English language. In Sanskrit the blowing out, extinguishing of a flame (a lamp), in Buddhism a state reached by the enlightened that is beyond birth and death, free of The Wheel of Life, samsara.

In common use in Australian English it is used as a superlative word to mean 'beyond worries', and commonly accepted in the first half of the Twentieth Century as a name to call one's house. (In contrast to Heaven)

In Buddhism it is not readily describable, because if you don't experience it you can't tell of it. I asked a lot of questions about it for a while (internally) and found it so confusing, and feeling myself such a novice, I gave up as a freshman would lose interest in an esoteric doctoral thesis.

However, it was somewhat relevant to my earlier questions about identity, and also my questions about a Buddhist who really comes to the "not I" position. What then? What is left?

Whatever it was, I was afraid of it: afraid because it was unknown; afraid because my 'I' wanted some sort of eternal continuity; afraid of what might happen next.

1982 extended into 1983. I had been sitting for almost three years, but looking back at where I was earlier, it had been most worthwhile.

In these years I read two American novels each by a distinguished author. One was E.L. Doctorow's Loon Lake, and the other Gore Vidal's 'Creation'.

Vidal's novel is set in the Fifth and Sixth Centuries BC. His protagonist Cyrus, as a significant functionary in the Persian Empire of Darius and later Xerxes, is to travel in that Empire, and to India, Bactria and Cathay. This is the time when the major religions of Asia have their era of initial development.

This protagonist, a grandson of Zoroaster, and preoccupied with Zoroaster's monotheistic deity, Ahura Mazdah, is taken to meet the Buddha personally.

While Vidal in a learned manner goes to much trouble to place the Buddha in historical context, he struggles with his perceptions. Some of this is clearly a skilled author's maintenance of his protagonist in character. It seems strange to Cyrus that the Buddha has been alive and has 'gone again', but here he is.
As an intensely thinking critic of major religion Vidal takes beliefs to the absurd to expose them to examination. He looks at the stories of the Vedic God Brahma's encounters with the Buddha, where the Buddha is confident

that Brahma should also seek relief from the cycle of birth and death, be mortal again as the only station from which such relief might be found.

While at one level bringing out that aspect of Buddhism that is outside the influence of gods, as his protagonist tells of it, Vidal exposes the supernatural implausibility in these 'encounters'.
Interestingly his protagonist Cyrus, at the end of the novel, says as 'a slip', that he wants to be restored "... to the primal unity." — then corrects himself with a Zoroastrian explanation.

This is also evident in Vidal saying bluntly that the Buddha has "gone again": he was alive but now he's dead, yet still there to be spoken to: without the curiosity about what that might mean, that preposterous assertion.

I found all of Vidal's novel highly stimulating. In a much later essay entitled 'Gods and Greens', he says in a postscript to a critique of monotheism, he says, "For Buddha, we are not here except to be gone from here."

Vidal set me thinking swiftly. The timing was appropriate — I mean that I had come some of the way.

The question arises: What remains after 'I' is recognised for an illusion? '

Mind' is certainly there, even if a motion, a process, but a 'no thing'. Does what is left have an identity? Vidal's notion is of the individual having been there and having gone. My immediate reaction to that: a change in perception, a knowing that 'what is', is only process of 'the always so'.

To paraphrase Descartes: "I think; thinking is a process: therefore, I am not." And: as Life is a process: the Buddha is Life itself.

Well, what identity to ascribe, to that which has always been there and yet is nothing at all, but for a while, was considered an entity, and named I or Juanita Abebe or Rajendra Smit or Thomas Skead, until awareness came as to what was there from the beginning. What is there? What is left? What identity has it? The Jungians ask similar questions, as false notions of 'I' are by-passed during the 'individuation' of Jungian therapy.

There wouldn't have been anybody to tell Vidal the answer to his questions. And anyway, he has left the question and gone. The impression I had was that he had dismissed it as some unexplainable mysticism or misleading semantic. I wanted neither of those; they spoke of an utter dead end, and this may be reflective of Vidal's understanding of Buddhism.
But what is left?

And this question wasn't an obscure one. It was about a state I could reproduce readily during zazen practice; it was about something I was sure of from my combined knowledge of neuroscience and the insight from *'The goose is out'*. The meaning of 'Buddha-nature' exemplifies it.

So is it valid to use the notion of 'identity' about 'what is left' at all? And it is not simply a question about Shakyamuni, but about every person — Vidal included.

Doctorow, in his novel Loon Lake features a character who goes to Japan to a Zen monastery, and through him satirises both the character and his experience.

The Master does not come through as a positively framed figure, and the event where 'the Buddhas in the hall' are overturned is depicted chaotically with no indications of its meaning. Zen is depicted as essentially Japanese and not readily translatable to a living experience for somebody outside Japanese culture.

But even considering that 'other culture' aspect, it is depicted as ordinary, and the character cannot stay with that. For all that, it was portrayed vividly and provocatively, and alongside Vidal, provided a balancing force to my preoccupations.

FEELINGS AND THE MIDDLE WAY

The Middle Way was a notion I liked as an image. Originally it meant taking a middle way between extreme asceticism and self-indulgence — from the beginning Buddhism was anti-extremist, anti-fundamentalist.

This was directly from Shakyamuni's own teaching and example. The bowl of rice milk at the critical point before his enlightenment is the focal scene. It is applicable in many spheres of conduct: it is not scrupulous or obsessive; it is tolerant of other religious beliefs. It creates levels of tolerance and flexibility in Buddhist meditation practices, religious observances and ethics.

This was helpful both in zazen practice and in coming to terms with the flow of emotional energy. Does a young man have more emotional energy to contain? Was that helpful or unhelpful? Where would the fear go? The fear of nirvana — whatever it was: and the other fears: — illness particularly. Where would the rage go?

I was only outwardly obedient. On the other hand, I knew I was directing more energy towards zazen practice, and as much again to my koan and endeavors to understand the nature of myself.

On the other hand so much more could be available if my feelings were suffered through, owned, transformed. I saw one way of this being brought about: by awareness taking me above pettiness. This was certainly a great benefit I'd gained during my own professional training as a result of supervision/therapy.

To Nagarjuna there was a middle way between 'being' and 'non-being', samsara and nirvana, Sunyatta and The Ten Thousand Things.

He brought complementarity and relativity to philosophy, as they were brought to physics about eighteen hundred years later.

SHIKAN TAZA

I had not chosen a new koan, as I was aware that my koan needed to become part of me, rather than just understood, and that I may have only found a middle level of it.

Also, I was still improving at my zazen practice, and having gained so much more from it that I'd ever suspected was possible, I still thought that more would come.

I was aware that the largest benefit had come from straight sitting with no koan being processed and no specific mindfulness. This is disciplining the mind to stop verbal sequential thought — more than that, to stop the concepts, the classifying — stay aware without all that, stay aware with no memory or anticipation, concentrate to the point of by-passing sensation.

I would bring this about regularly by the combination of hands, eyes, breathing, focus beneath the navel, and the initial use of the image of a mirror. I would develop an image of a mirror in space. It had a concave surface, and out there in one direction would be stars. The mirror turned away from the stars and became 'nothing' seeing nothing.

With some experience, all this malarky is quite unnecessary, and it was fortunate the 'mirror' was allowed to disappear and the awareness — no boundary,

Indeed, this 'mirror strategy' which arose from imaging techniques is to be directly discouraged as it could lead to misunderstanding and obstruction of zazen/prajna.

'Not I', came to be zazen itself. My eyes no longer dried then became full of tears. My blink reflex acquired a regularity like breathing.

To communicate the wakeful awareness of nothing, witnessing what the nervous system is doing without thinking in the usual sense, must be experienced: it cannot be described.

This type of zazen practice (without the imaging) is called *shikan taza*.

Utstein Kloster

During 1983 I went to a conference on helping the victims of disasters. It was held at Utstein Kloster in South Western Norway. This was a very old monastery built on an island in a fjord, where in ancient times had been the seat of early kings of Norway.

It had a strange ambience for me, as it was midsummer. The sun set only for a few hours and then left a calm twilight. I had been reading Kristen Lavransdatter (The novel by Nobel Prize winning author of the late Twenties, Sigrid Undset) which left me with a view and feeling for Norway that went beneath appearances.

Two of the staff, who were from English speaking countries, talked to me, and without my giving them any outward message of my own that I was aware of, in a natural manner told me about their conversion to Buddhism. This included a commitment to tolerance and peace, both important issues to them. It also included a strong sense of belief in and wishes for rebirth.

I did not disclose anything of myself verbally; I accepted their confidence fully. It threw me back on my own unresolved development. I was certainly different in viewpoint from them. How?

It was to do with 'the oneness', my loss of being a 'subject' to the not me 'objects'. That applied to people. I was them. All part of the oneness. I saw clearly the that's all there is now oneness, registered in my nervous system now oneness, was not separate from the once and future oneness or the absolute oneness/ everything that included Galaxy M31.

Born again? Yes! Inevitably! But existing now, in contemporaries: — the lack of boundary became more meaningful, and a new view of the world was forming. How can that fit into ordinary life? Be accepted?

And what were the implications? What is left when 'I' is known as an illusion? And what of its nature?

Vidal's next question? I could sit with the question. Breath with it.

I found that whatever had frightened me about nirvana was gone, but I still had no idea what nirvana meant. For one thing I was still full of 'I'. Take me into any familiar context and my understandings were skin-deep, or at least they existed beside untamed feelings when my 'I' was thwarted; and I still had contradictory senses of identity. and was still dominated by the habits of subject and object duality.

Development IV

I came away from Utstein Kloster with strong feelings of sadness; my life had changed. I had to accept the way my major relationships were.

I would also adapt to the new way I saw everything.

DEVELOPMENT V

Development V

Around a Small Star

This time was one of growing awareness, getting to know: — The Everything, the teaching, 'what was left when 'I' had gone' that goes beyond time and space, sometimes called in Buddhist writing 'The always so'. Küng calls it 'The unnamed God of the Buddhists'. Küng has his point of view.

The physicist might say that it is matter/energy/spacetime changing, being its essential *'neither wave nor particle'* virtual face, creating interesting and useful illusions as the nervous system changes with intricate process as part of it.

Some Buddhists might say The Everything has 'Buddha nature' and it is its essence that is seen.

Teilhard talks of God evolving, which is a result of aspects of process — a God of 'matter' — the real world.

The similarities between all of these come more to the foreground than the differences.

Teilhard knew man was riding the changes of his species: never static, never completed, but had the hope that man would gain a spiritual and ethical unity where the Christic would be experienced by all. To him, man was on the way.

Küng and Teilhard both want the Judeo-Christian tradition to grow up and thus survive. Undoubtedly it will evolve to be broadly consistent with what is known of the Universe: and survive without the supernatural. But it has problems other than supernaturalism.

A great difficulty will be anthropocentrism: the view or belief that Man is at the centre of everything: evolution, the Universe, Buddha nature, the planet Earth, ecology.

Yet, in only a few centuries, we have been able to bear that the Earth is not the centre of the Universe, that it rotates around the sun, a small star in the spiral arm of a galaxy containing a hundred billion other stars at least; and that's not one of the big ones like M104.

Not only that, but the sun's 66-million-year orbit around the galactic centre roughly 20,000 light years away, takes it about 250 light years 'above' the plane of 'The Milky Way' and a similar distance 'below'. And, there are as many galaxies known as there are stars in our own galaxy.

On this planet are some millions of species of organism. All of them evolving, interdependent, but competing, changing to be as they will be.

Zoology and ecology give us no evidence of any central biological role for man, only of being a temporarily successful organism at taking over a variety of environments, creating the usual pressures of overpopulation that leads to decline as the habitat is destroyed or befouled.

And yet from homo sapiens' point of view, what the human nervous system does, becomes a focus of our sense of marvel. From my earlier insights as a young man: knowing that you and me, and feeling and sensitivity, come from all this — to look at the nature of the common chemical elements and how they go together to make things as they are: truly marvelous.

What to call it?

Development V

THE TAO

Just as imaginary experiments in an imaginary elevator were germinal to relativity, somebody put an imaginary gosling in a glass jar some twelve centuries ago — she's out — and the implications are reverberating down the years from China to Japan to The West.

Suzuki was a rich source of information about the development of Zen in China. Robert Aitken vitally demonstrates the life of the old masters. Here was a collision between Buddhism and Taoism: Zen — a hybrid evolved from the better qualities of both.

The pragmatic Chinese attitudes to life, telling it how it is, the revival of Buddhism back to its source by The Sixth Patriarch Hui-nêng, but with a fresh and strong direction derived from the vital but immaterial Tao — only Tao. These factors gave Zen the impetus that has carried Buddhist life to us over a further thirteen centuries.

The Tao te Ching gives a view.

I am surrounded by the influence of the Tao te Ching, in that I was familiar with it in the years immediately before my attention was directed to Zen. My attention comes back to it again.

The Tao te Ching, referring to 'The Tao' in XlV,

"it is nameless and in ceaseless motion":

All of XlV expresses 'The always so'.

Is 'the process of the everything', 'the way of the everything', the Tao of the Tao te Ching, 'The always so' of Zen, Küng's 'Unnamed God of the Buddhists': are these all ways of expressing the ... ?

There are credible pantheists such as Teilhard who see the significance of process beside the 'substance' of the Universe, and are seeing it as a oneness, a whole, and as such, as an entity — in Teilhard's perspective, God: immanent in, or suffusing 'The Everything', evolving within the collective consciousness of Man.

Kung's divine being is in everything too, but more than the collective consciousness of men and women, the quality is not directly known: is indescribable and not to be compared with a human.

Development V

While it may seem to be a matter of semantics, there is essential difference in Buddhist perception. Küng may say of The Absolute that He is timeless and Total, but the implication is Somebody.

A Buddhist sees wondrous process — Quality-energy, the process of processes in all its forms ... but Nothing, not Somebody.

Yet there is your experience Now?

THE WRIGGLING EEL

Including this, I was still confused. Words, arguments, more philosophising: whenever I'm recreating my thinking around Teilhard and Küng, or using capital letters, I'm doing some variety of verbal sword-play.

I had some idea within me about the 'All this', but I'd had it since I was a young man in my early twenties: all the constipated thinking that was going on since then, even including my awareness of unity with everything else, and my feeling for Mind, they didn't fit together.

Rumi the Sufi saw wordy efforts to define spiritual reality as facing away from and avoiding the Reality of 'Not I'.

I could remember Suzuki quoting Shakyamuni himself likening this thinking, to *the wriggling of an eel*, of which there are modern equivalents.

Rage and Reality

Science has had to depart from logic and develop expressions for uncertainty, chaos and complementarity — leading most often to probabilities and/or alternatives.

I also knew from my own professional training and practice that intuition was a valid manner of assessment — often the only was to deal with a highly complex situation. Moreover, I knew that intuition was not magic, or exclusive female wisdom, but true, and less likely to mistake the words for the bread.

Intuition is a function of a specialised part of the brain that perceives as a whole. It had been well studied and was the foundation of Gestalt Psychology and Kellyan psychology.

Long before I was interested in Zen, I had supervised field workers in associated professions; they would be assessing an issue of potential safety for a child; it was difficult for them to formulate in words reasons indicating the dangerst o a child in a projected future, when, for example, the child would be in a specific person's custody. I would bring them back to their intuitive sense.

The most able ones would have a strong and rich intuitive perception, not only from their own point of view but from the child's. Then we would work backwards from that. Difficult work because it is easily contaminated by themes from their own or colleagues' deeper fears.

What were the detailed observations that went to that intuition? What was their significance? It was dissecting perfectly sound intuition and making it less meaningful, but it was going to enable us to put that child's position to people trained in the law, to whom our intuition would be mostly meaningless and before whom the child was powerless.

I had consciously worked in that way since 1970. Sometimes the dissection of my intuition, turning it over for evidence, would give me a closer view and change the overall intuitive assessment: that way I had the best of both. But I was conscious too of destroying the intuited sense when I did that.

Yet my view of the dharma was still verbal, logical, skeptical. True, it subsumed my intuitive grasp of *'The goose is out'*, but even that was floating around in a soup of words and propositions that was confusing. The suffering reader will know immediately.

Then I had an insight of another type, of which the psychotherapist reader would have been aware before page twenty, indeed the paper chase has

Development V

obvious clues for the discerning reader. Indeed, the synthesist of self will follow it all the way, while the analyst will draw conclusions about my not accepting supernaturalism. It was an insight familiar from earlier development of self, and where I go with my adult patients in a general sense.

The realisation: I was very angry: so distrustful about an understanding of the world. I was an enraged child who had been sensitive to magic, frightened by it.

I had been disillusioned, and as a child and young adult had a strong, sense of the beliefs around me leading to foolish motives and the wasting of others' lives.

In wanting truth, and to share truth in daily living, I had been left feeling depressed and without direction.

I was furious in a hidden way: I wasn't going to accept another view of the Uni- verse and my place in it, without extreme caution.

Why I'd got this far, but only this far, was because I'd taken all the initiative and taken it alone, developed only what I had selected, out of simple angry distrust. Here was a core of rage that affected every aspect of my being.

I had insight into Teilhard's place in the world too, and for all my feeling closer to him, knew his insight was his, and why I could not accept it second hand.

And the koan? I think that recreating the scene of the original encounter is helpful: in this case between Nansen and 'the military man'. While weeding, it was going through my thoughts and Nansen says, *'The goose is out'*, on the "Out", or rather the 't' at the end of it, and then it stops: that was everything.

Mind was the sound, the silence, as it was the wall earlier.

And Now was nothing ... and 'Infinity'

After this there was not quite as much eel wriggling. Yet I knew I still had not grasped what I sought, and 'saw' only brief unconnected images.

Development V

The House in the garden

Nineteen eighty-four changed to 1985. I was not in a hurry. From what I'd understood at Utstein Kloster my life had changed. The farm had given way to a house in the city. During the three months there, I only did my opportunistic sitting in aircraft, alone in the office, or on steps and low walls.

The red-brick house in the garden changed all that. As the garden and I came to know one another, I realised there was a problem of communication about the dharma.

If it could be readily communicated, would not the world know it and live accordingly? There would be wider understanding of the manner in which wanting material things, wanting control over others and the events of living, these would lead to suffering.

Instead of desire would be hope, the intuitive awareness of some good enough virtual outcomes, not the hope that craving would be satisfied, or the hope that suffering would be extinguished in some magic fashion.

No, it was the hope to know how to live, the hope that insight and awareness would make what to do obvious. And to communicate that to others? How would they grieve their unfulfilled desires? How would they see it for themselves? To communicate across pain and grief?

What I would have said about it then, was that I thought it was an overall picture, something that would be 'seen' rather than concluded, and known as an intuitive whole, to do with 'the nature of everything', the movement, changing, processes of everything: an everything of which you and I are part.

Like science, various schools of Buddhism have developed their own language to communicate their experience and their connection to it. And here am I trying to adapt to one of them that required a lot of personal growth on my part. And I am telling that in the hope that a confused child could ever want adherence to a world view that was called a religion.

Development V

THE VIEW FROM ZAZEN

When experienced — zazen gives a view.

"This is all there is, there is nothing else", as known/experienced in zazen: it is Mind: the view is three-dimensional and no-dimensional and seems inexorably held captive by the fourth, becoming and becoming and becoming: process all of it, changing, developing.

This view — 'seeing' — unites it all: the 'no thing' that cannot gather dust. Nothing — and yet all the processes Mind might undergo are there.

The table is the table, is me, you, matter/energy/spacetime, all in motion: wave/particle in flux, the most stable being the standing waves of captive electrons, or the dance of a quark with its two partners.

'The Everything' changes, there are processes and processes — and eventually after four billion years of evolution on this planet, the process knows.

But, as a process — is nothing. Yet the nature of this 'nothing self' is obvious, and zazen itself is the way to seeing it all together. The 'seeing it all together' and zazen are one and the same.

And to think I'd had the hope that zazen would be so much value as a state of mind, and, while true, it trivializes.

The experience of zazen is where you find the nature of 'It all' directly, so much more than any sublime state of mind: confrontation with Self: yet with zazen 'the nothing' is peace, and 'emptiness' is experienced like the space inside a coil spring.

A tale

The adult teenager had bravely entered therapy. She trusts her therapist enough to say how it is. She doesn't like herself; and she is able to show her irritable resentful feelings.

"The Walkman helps — fills up my head. I hate changing tapes — I feel empty when it stops."

She must have seen an expression.

"You think that's okay?" She studied the calm woman's face to chase the meaning. It was a bright encouraging look she'd seen. Her therapist said. "An experiment. Let it happen — the empty bit; we'll be quiet for a minute."

The younger woman looked anxious, restless, but cooperated.

After about a minute she said, "Stupid! Just the printer and that silly bird."

The currawong gave one of it its less melodious social calls.

"Yes. That's right."

"And what I see every time."

"Everybody's like that, but not many know. All sorts of interesting things happen within it."

> *She will go on to know more about herself, her character, strengths and decision processes, her feeling quality and relating capacity, but she may also be able to use the very emptiness of which she is so afraid, if only for peace.*

Development V

"Resistance is Grief: Grief is Resistance"

There is a resistance then to receiving even clear communication of the dharma.

In sitting was the zazen experience, simple and true: compared with the experience of all Mind would hold at once, even if confused — 'All this' — everyday mind.

Then back to zazen, the simplicity of 'Just this'. They were not essentially different. The comparison became uppermost in consideration for many weeks. There was much opportunity to compare the zazen experience with many samples of 'All this '.

The process of 'All this' was obvious in its finer state (zazen), when the confusion, clutter and striving were gone. The subject/object unity was true and the sense of it all being Mind was total.

But there was much to lose — the whole culture's wishes and beliefs about satisfactions for the individual, for one.

All the shared defensive strategies to foster self-importance and hold off awareness of pain, ignorance and decay- for two.

The resistance to 'seeing' was the resistance to giving up all the egocentric wish-fulfilment that the culture offered.

Both the 'Tao te Ching', and 'In Memoriam' come to mind immediately: the latter's

She cries *"a thousand types are gone:*
I care for nothing, all shall go."

And the Tao's likening man's position to that of 'straw dogs' (or 'straw offerings' in other translations). There is a hint of the same grief in both.

Tennyson's grief at his friend's death became a vehicle for his grief at the nature of the world as he saw it from Victorian England.

His lines from the mouth of Nature, represented the division of his Nineteenth Century world: God and Nature: confusion, a painful struggle for meaning. What position has The Creator to the world? How to adapt to the shocking new understanding of that time — the implications of 'evolution'?

Despite the author of the Tao te Ching not personifying the Tao, the use of 'straw offerings' to express the position of individual creatures is an expression of human grief, even if of a grief that has been resolved.

Tennyson's grief was anything but resolved.

Tennyson was struggling for hope in all this. Was man simply caught up in this process of evolution? And where does 'right' and 'wrong', 'good' and 'evil' get caught up in this ceaseless change with countless outcomes?

The 'straw dogs', the extinction of species, are not separate from The Tao, The Dharma, they accompany it, are part of it. And 'good', 'evil', 'right', 'wrong' are values, important values from the viewpoint taken by a particular aspect of The Dharma. As the Buddha saw in the suffering of others the desires of 'I - ness' would bring more hurt upon the sufferer. He would show them how to prevent such suffering.

But to go that way?

I was aware in an intellectual manner that the ultimate grief was in letting 'I' itself go — falling off the cliff, climbing higher than the top of the pole: that was where the resistance was caught in a knot.

Development V

SITTING ZEN

There was now a change developing in my zazen practice. There was a great difference when I was sitting with my awareness of *'no thing' that cannot 'gather dust'*, becoming used to the Zazen/'seeing' experience that was not to be lost.

What was there when 'I' had gone — and without boundaries — was unmistakable.

I was also aware zazen was pervading my everyday life, at some times more than others. If I wished, I was more aware of it. On the other hand, if I introduced mindfulness into zazen, I would lose this sense of Mind, and even though uncluttered, my focused thought would chuff away like a train in a quiet landscape.

Then I became aware that my struggling with the koan would go much better while weeding the garden or driving on the highway. Zazen style of mindfulness had generalised and seemed to flow.

And I was sure there was more in the goose. The goose was part of the everything too. I was the goose.

She processed things from her world, and so did I. I made goose noises while weeding around the trunk of the mango tree.

The goose hadn't been taught to conceptualise an 'I', inside, outside. My skin or skull didn't limit me but who was, what was ... ? What I was being was still intellectual, wordy. Or some bit of it was.

Each day I would pass a flock of geese on my way to work and my sharing of their nature was more than words.

One Friday morning in April 1987, I was driving from one place where I worked to another: it was a long drive and I had started about seven or eight minutes previously. I was thinking about koan generally, and the manner in which the goose had come to dominate my thinking until I was feathers, when 'The one hand' came to mind:

The sound of one hand clapping. Then: 'seeing' simply happened.

You would have seen tears stream down my face — feeling, happy tears, and the words came "May it keep on clapping"; the silliness of which was obvious, and was indeed a contrast to 'seeing'.

'Seeing', was intimate recognising, no more than that, but it remained un- dimmed. The overwhelming sense of clapping: empty, open, changing, process - and nothing else, that was some of it:

'The Sound' perceiving itself: One, timeless, indestructible, and without boundary. Family was still family, work was still work, teeth to be cleaned, dishes to wash.

Who sat at the lights at the southern end of the shopping centre? Who was there from the beginning?

Who reads this?

Name as you will: Dhyana, 'the everything', Mind, Tao, 'The always so', "Wu!" the Chinese nothingness, Sunyatta, 'Now', 'The Sound of One Hand Clapping', Reality, all of those - how misleading are the labels we give and accept. The dark glass is words.

DEVELOPMENT VI

YES

The children grew; the trees grew, work grew. After the stunned effect, so did the smiles, warm surprises at the new view of everyday. So did the pain: the distress available at work or through the media, seemed vast. The clear awareness that they were as they were, while preventing inappropriate or foolish action, did not limit the pain. That The Sound was always in action, helped too.

Initially 'seeing' was the awareness of incredible smallness. The body — a flicker in development of the species that is approaching a critical level of overpopulation on a small but beautiful planet, apparently unable to save itself, perhaps one of billions of species in the change upon change upon change.

And contrition was engulfing. A conviction of not repeating acts leading to bad karma was reassuring. In some areas reparation or even undoing was possible. 'Seeing', was to have awareness of colossal ignorance.

The experience was to seem like powerlessness itself, but it was neither power nor powerlessness because The Sound without boundary was Action itself. And The Sound here: indivisible: what was here always ... recognised.

But simple smallness, this eddy in the wind, saw the momentum of change and the huge complexity and unpredictability of The Way.

Encouraging was the parable of the mustard seed. That the effects of Right Action were circular and expanding was also encouraging, also that good karma brought further good outcome, and Right Action broke the circular swirl of bad karma. As ethical conviction develops and spreads, The Sound is trusted as The Great Way.

Clear also were the attempts of others to understand their world. They would take a view and adapt to the influences that impinged on them Whatever their position, it was to be respected as their security, comfort and rest.

Development VI

Replenishment

At first, sitting helped to adapt to the stunned effect. This effect would not take any shape. But what was there — Self was sufficient, on the way, all over, as if 'Small view Thomas' had become 'Wide view Thomas' in an inevitable manner.

Sitting became a replenishment of resources, or a natural pleasure. Yet the utter necessity of sitting for development was confirmed. And so was the essence of sitting: developing awareness without words, observation without 'I', concentration without senses.

This was quite different from 'meditating on a subject', the counterpart of which happened while gardening, showering, walking or driving.

The experience of sitting was first hand Self. Sitting was being the truth. What is called 'conscious': a small wave upon the vast Not-conscious: upon Nothing, seen clearly, but it was only one experience of this among others. This was because the zazen experience was in all living. It was easier with simple activities, but experiencing One/Now while with others was still undeveloped.

The wise master will say, "It is not from the one hand but the endeavour at *'The goose is out'*." While that is true, the 'clapping' is pivotal, the 'sound' is pivotal, the 'hand' is pivotal, and 'one' is pivotal, the 'one hand' is pivotal and every combination of all of those is pivotal, and perceiving the sound of one hand clapping is all.

Now The Goose owns the glass jar and is caring for her feathers despite her 'problem', and all is comfortable. True, she is astounded at the number and beauty of her feathers, her size and talents - she can even miaow and bark: "Wu!" She means what she says.

Once a senior monk had pointed at an aspirant, asking, "Who carries that bag of bones through the world?", as a koan. The memory came back with laughter at the clarity now experienced.

But there was an awareness: in order to find this, there had been a journey to an area of perception where acceptable sanity left no marks, where sincere communication with peers would be bizarre and incomprehensible, where coexistence of the illusory and the aware points of view was necessary, and the container for all of it - efficient.

The sense of gratitude to Shakyamuni was pervasive. It was Shakyamuni the searcher, the striver, the effort taker. Two and a half thousand years ago without the benefit of Twentieth Century knowledge: to be awake, aware, to show its effects and implications. The first time?

Yet Shakyamuni would have it that there had been many others aware before, and he was those others: the experience: oneness — non-discrimination, survival of 'that which is awake'.

The gratitude surging through, carrying the detritus of thought, while seeming an aspect of 'I': and treating Shakyamuni as another 'I', was not that.

Making a fable of The Goose version of what had happened would go something like this:

> The man knows the view from the summit of the mountain is very important. There are others going there. He can see where the ground starts to rise, but he realises it is a difficult mountain to gauge, because of the changes in viewpoint. The terrain here is bleak and unfeatured and covered with rounded pebbles.
>
> He walks around the base to the right, and, on one side, finds a temple with many monks and nuns. With calm concentration they are going about their daily work. There is smoke coming from the kitchen, washing on the line, and the garden is well tended.
>
> He walks further around until he comes to the opposite side; there is a steep and difficult slope and many people tackling this slope rapidly, but others coming down again looking tired. Strangely they were attended by some fruit-bats who would seem to know where the climber would pause.
>
> On the third side was another monastery, but on looking at it more closely it was some sort of school or college. There was a rotating dome for a telescope and a large dish antenna. It had big gates, but there was no barrier to anybody who wished to go onto the slope.
>
> He went further around the base, until he came back to where he'd started. As good a place as any to start?
>
> Approaching the first pinch, the loose round pebbles gave way under his feet. He had thought it looked easy, but it was difficult to see each hazard until he came to it. The shoes were a disadvantage; and he hadn't brought the right equipment.
>
> He had to stop and look at his hands and his feet, and then to try

Development VI

and see as much of the mountain as he could, but all that was there was rolling loose pebbles. But he saw a tuft of grass, and inside his shoes he had toes.

Climbing a little, his newly discovered toes felt good digging into the slope. Here were some little trees; they helped him further until he came to a straight rock wall. There was a message cut into it with a chisel. 'Climb downwards' it said.

He decided to go to the left above the College, and after climbing downwards for some time, the nature of the slope changed. There were other climbers there. One was taking photographs of the slope, while another was brushing at a spot on the climbing face with a tiny camel-hair brush.

This slope had larger rocks, and if dislodged they would cause injury.

Now, whenever he found an easy way around a promising corner, anticipating a clear way to the top, it ended in a sheer drop or an outcrop. On the other hand, despite a prickly bush that brought him out in a rash, it was as it was.

At one point he looked onto the steep slope on the other side of the mountain, and there was a middle-aged woman climbing it, making the use of every tiny hold. Her fruit bat flew behind her soundlessly. She smiled at him from across the slope.

Instead of joining her he went back to his original slope and had a good look at it.

There were still the rolling mini-boulders and the loose surface, but he looked carefully at this slope and its plants and animals. He must be above the steep wall that had stopped him earlier. There was more grass, and a flock of geese was grazing on it. He crossed their meadow, interested in the way they ate the short green grass, steadily one blade and then the next one.

Around the corner of the mountain on the slope above the monastery was a monk sitting calmly on a rock. He didn't look up from his meditation for quite a while. He did not seem to be going   anywhere. At last the monk spoke warmly in an unintelligible language, but his presence said much more. Then he smiled.

The climber had a feeling as if he was sitting there smiling too. Seriously he wondered who he was. Now he looked to his friends the footholds and his friends the trees who showed him the way.

He wondered when he found the geese at his next easier pinch. They may have flown: do domestic geese fly? Yet, up towards the summit they had come nonetheless.

He gave up climbing. He stayed with them and the grass and trees until feathers and femaleness and childhood were natural. It was much easier to go onto the other slopes now.

The Monk was still there sitting in meditation even closer to the summit, and at the steep slope there was a goat nimbly crossing it with obvious curiosity. The goose pushed the limb of her orange tree towards the goat, who ate the orange, skin and all.

She spread her wings and felt like flying but was surprised how big she was, her wings seemed to cover the mountain and there she was at the summit, and it was gone. And he/she was more than a goose. Stardust for feathers: and nothing but wings beating.

To say it in everyday language, 'The man' always thought about it as 'The Summit', but it was a summit and not so high at all, but his original idea of wanting to go there for what he'd see was right.

In front is a series of peaks going upwards to the mist; the terrain is visible yet the difficulties major, and the valley that must be crossed to climb to the other peaks is crowded with all the creatures of the world living their destiny — some trying to climb towards his peak.

Yet he must go to the mountains leading up into the mist. All the myriad creatures are brothers and sisters and the path for them through the high mountains must be made.

Yet he is a novice, inept for the next part of the journey, remembers being a 'Private, recruit minor' in the days when he'd put down his rifle. This body: a small barnacle on 'Eternity'. It was like that. But what was necessary was clearer now the view was there.

There was nothing but the 'Now', and the 'Now' was everything, but altogether. Yet he was dressed in old habits. Habits of

Development VI

separateness, habits with walls, 'now' and 'then' habits, intolerant habits, unloving habits, disrespectful habits, even the habit of craving to have no habits. Here was the beginning of learning.

Much of it would be negative capability — unlearning, putting the dross aside.

And it is difficult to know the hostile, the cruel and the detached as One. It was all down there in the valley. It could not be anything else. There was no convenient split into 'the goodies' and 'the baddies': 'The everything' being as it was. It is difficult to know anger and fear as energy: energy that is compassionate action.

It is difficult to perceive all the relative 'good' and 'bad' in the action of the world and grieve that it is as it is. But to foster its salvation, engage it, whatever the sequence of joy and suffering, will be done: ineptly at first: the apprentice has much to learn. The 'illusion in the works' gone, 'Not I' is open, involved, and has prodigious energy.

The Transmutation of 'I'

'I', even after the second look, was still an issue.

There is much confusion between the 'I' identity and 'the self': the latter is the process of perceiving widely, marrying feeling and thought, these processes organised for action — Now.

Arjuna received this clear message from The Blessed Lord Krishna.

Not only was there survival of the dynamic self, but without the delusion 'I', the self was fortified. This was 'self' recognised as one of the myriad processes of 'not I': 'Self', 'The Sound', 'Absolute Self'.

In contrast 'I' was unmasked. It was 'I' who wanted, who 'deserved' or was 'entitled'. 'I' carried fear and anger from the past. 'I' was the mission for power and success, and all the pretenses around its failure. 'I' was the repository of greed and insecurity. There was not enough money or land or health or life.

'I' was the belief in the somebody — somebody particular, who, in unconscious fantasy, is central, unchanging, needy, discounted and deprived. 'I' is subject to status and status struggle among the family, peers and society. The social ascriptions define 'I' and fix 'I' in a gel of words and images. 'I' concentrates on the opinion of others, ponders, waits and has many reasons yet does little.

Initially, Thomas doubting was from an 'I' position, as if at another 'I': "Countless people thought they knew the meaning of the one hand?

Could it be expressed to somebody who really knew? Could you even begin to grasp its implications? Do you know anything about the one hand? You've been struggling with 'that goose' in its bottle for almost eight years and followed it every- where; you know nothing of the one hand. It's not even your koan. You get to tussle with a koan until you are the koan, and here you are, a few perfunctory thoughts about another one and you know?"

In contrast the 'seeing' was there. Whatever the doubts, it was simply there. It was totally embracing; it had a simple sense of identity and an unhampered self. Compare this with the 'intellectual understanding' approach in 'The Ridge Pole' which starts in Development III, page 71, where there is 'philosophy' and no'sight' at all, apart from the last few lines.

Certainly, no awareness of Self. But it had been necessary to grieve that 'I' was a figment of wishes from the smorgasbord presented by the culture, or an illusion for the species to survive and evolve.

Yet the survival of 'I' was more than persistence of habits. It should not have been as surprising. However surely 'I' was illusion, it could be observed waving the flag of its identity, fulfilling its own prophecies, following the suggestions of its culture. Here was the suggestibility of everyday life, the tie to cause and effect in all meanings of 'cause and effect'.

Inevitable for each one, is the struggle with his own narcissism. Concerted struggle provides the opportunity to understand its nature. This is helped considerably when the illusion is penetrated.

Rumi spending a long and detailed effort in identifying 'I' and then pushing it aside to experience enlightenment was a contrast to the New Age assertion of those who have learnt the false syllogism: "God is expressed through people: therefore 'I' am God" to give their omnipotence an ultimate boost and bring disrespect to new religious thinking.

While the 'I' remnants are fragments, and seem as blatant as a confident child manipulating an adult towards a desired outcome, they were to be 'seen' and offered no encouragement. There was also the issue that these remnants had diminished over the years since taking a positive focus on true self.

But the surprise at 'I's survival was only an initial reaction: 'I' would be gradually superseded. The functioning self simply leaves 'I' behind. 'I' mostly goes off on tangents — wordy ones at that. The self accustomed to zazen thinks/ feels what is necessary, moves on, does some more, takes executive action — it is the stuff of leadership, whereas 'I' is a dragging anchor.

'Seeing' not only brought tender laughter, but relief from pain and striving. It is not easy to describe such relief. It did not come all at once, but time after time when action was easy, effective and uncomplicated. 'I' preoccupations were exposed like small dreams in the morning, and zazen cleared confusion rapidly.

'Not I'. His insight was the convergence of zen and some mainstreams of psychotherapy: particularly those therapies which look to an unencumbered self, and those directed to adult wholeness — more integrative than analytic.

While zazen is not a replacement for the 'work' of therapy, it surely makes the experience of self clear and works in the same direction, making the unnecessary 'I clutter' obvious.

Some who practice zazen may find psychotherapy of use to expose the unowned or hidden aspects of personality that might play status games or be closed to the pain of others.

Within Western society there is a diverse but capable group, some of whose members avail themselves of therapies and a few of zen development. Within a society hungry for 'a way' and confused by the media, what responsibility do the privileged or fortunate have to bring benefits to their broader society? How might they deliver practical contact to those interested?

To Asians who can go to their Buddhist priest or community elder for support, Buddhism in Western countries must seem strange indeed.

Externally the differences would develop slowly. No magic signs would appear.

The evening meal would be enjoyed: the singing to the two-year-old would be the same: the warm laughter was containable. She went to sleep usually before "Bloomin' idol made of mud" because it was well into the second verse.

From Self the view was different immediately. The issue is that there was an experience that 'Not I' was all that was real.

Without knowing anything of the experimental results of Twentieth Century Science, Shakyamuni, Rumi, the Taoist sages, and the authors of the Upanishads were fully aware of the process nature of 'The always so', particularly this aspect of Mind.

Thinking back to the illusion produced by cinematography, and then to the great illusions inherent in the finely tuned complex between the ears: these great illusions are' I', 'time' and 'something' — the illusion of 'something' implying permanence. And it wasn't even 'I' and 'time' and 'something', but rather 'I/time/something' that was the illusion.

Development VI

On Illusions

Part of 'seeing' is that in eating a bun, you place it in your mouth and bite it, next you chew it. How does Mind perceive anything, considering the body's processes are in sequence?

Yet the pictures painted in perception: they span the dimension of experience we call time: are at least four dimensional. So the time canvas can take the colour of the grass and sky.

There was wonder that perception could hold so much from the sensory stimuli received, despite the awareness that Utter Oneness spans many dimensions naturally. The physics and neuroscience of this cannot be kept out of the new questions to be asked or the ensuing thought.

The next six pages are about the coming together of zen and a science viewpoint of Mind. Considering it is 'thick' reading even to revise it — a jump to 'Change' on page 136 could be appropriate.

The Twentieth Century has been a time of crisis for the physicist, as mass, energy and spacetime have come to be viewed as faces of the same basic process of the Universe.

The physicist sees the 'solidity' of matter as the resistance of the standing waves of 'orbiting' electrons to the standing waves of other electrons. They see the particles of the tiny atomic nucleus as energy concentrations undergoing countless processes, interchanges, to be perceived as mass.

The notion of 'particle': — itself a convention to describe a process in the void. A physicist might ask, "What is special about the quantum mechanics of a nervous system compared with a stone? Do the particles behave according to another mode of existence?"

There have been some outstanding popular accounts of the parallels between the conclusions of the sages, and those of Twentieth Century physicists. Despite their different methods and the millennia that separate Shakyamuni and Lao Tzu on one hand and Einstein and Bohr on the other, they are similar.

Considering the commonalities: observation of natural experiment and eschewing wishful thinking: is their difference of method more than superficial?

The knowing of time became much clearer. When Now of meditation and of everyday experience is known, the confusion once experienced, deserves explanation.

There are various views of 'now' and 'time':

Of 'now':

There is Now of zazen, a close acquaintance with Now of everyday experience, except, being united and uncluttered, its nature is not confusing. 'Time/change maps' on page 133 addresses this further.

The 'now' of language usage, which may mean "Nineteen ninety-six", "during this conversation", or, "this football match is 'coming through live'", or , "we are discussing 'this moment' ".

The 'now' of physics: always some milliseconds 'before' any 'now' of the nervous system. (The 'start' of time measurement) Inseparable matter/ energy/ spacetime when considered by physics, has dimensions. The dimensions are part of the observer.

But as one observer may be subject to a different gravitational field and have a different velocity to another, the time dimension might be relatively contracted or expanded, and events simultaneous to one observer might not be to another. Such is Einstein's Universe, but not Newton's.

And 'time':

Movement/change goes on; time is the movement/change, as also are length and breadth and depth. Time does not fly, march or evaporate. Corresponding movement occurs in the nervous system too, and this may be set against regular movement such as the movement of pendulums and vibrating crystals.

But 'now' when cut to minuscule quantities of such comparisons is very hard to find. The search reveals nothing at all. This view of time may be understood abstractly — and it might be 'reality', yet it is not Reality.

Perceived time: the nervous system by its presence and function participates in the order of each and every movement and gives time apparent direction.

Without this function, that is, the wave of depolarisation of the nerve cell axon going in one direction as a trail of gunpowder lit at one end, keeping the neuronal net active in its maps and patterns, time would not appear to pass in Now.

We could take this further and consider many axes of time which might be conceived: Stephen Hawking writes of 'imaginary time' at varying degrees to our perceived axis of time.

Also consider the symmetry of time, including 'anti-matter' being as 'matter' moving on a 180 degree axis (backwards) in time: for example the positron being an electron doing just this. And consider that every photon moving in a vacuum loses its garb or immediately leaves our axis.

Taking the anthropic principle once more, but on this occasion applied to time axes: the electrically charged cylinder (nerve axon) depolarising in a wave in one direction and the synaptic nerve junction adapted to carrying the impulse in one direction only, means that however many axes 'time' might have and however photons or quasars may move in them, the human nervous system will perceive the Universe from the axis in which its nerve impulse conduction functions.

Thus, it has its own perhaps unique experience of movement. We can observe directly the effects of differing speeds of nervous system function in the dragonfly and the giant tortoise. Such differences are easy to conceive when they have the same vector, but in another?

What is experienced is relative movement: the speed and direction of movement of the nervous system set off against that of another process. Direct experience is limited: the mating of the dragon-fly and the growing of the cedar are outside it.

Time is a dimension, an abstraction. It quantifies by the movement 'nervous system' comparing two other movements (the swimmer and the stopwatch), and that comparison has assumptions about 'beginning', direction and 'end'. So, all time is imaginary in the sense of being subjective. Beyond the illusion is the Timeless.

And that which is Movement/Change can be mapped by Itself. One apparent dimension of it is called 'time'.

Time/change maps

When the illusion of 'time' is known, the similarity to knowing about other illusions such as 'I' will be appreciated.

'The always so' has evolved not only life, but complex organisms with a nervous system that can make 'time/change maps' of all sizes:

For example, a map of the sequence of sounds made by the vocal apparatus in enunciating serially the 'mm', 'a' and 'p' sounds of the word 'map'. It can be re-created whenever its meaning is required. Examples of maps built up from serial events are readily available to mind. But the representations are organised to be experienced whole across many milliseconds - a bridge from one movement to others, uniting them along the dimension called time.

This sensory memory and its implications are so taken for granted that few wonder how the world would seem without it.

There are also maps that make the illusion of 'I' possible by being the neural representation of an individual's life and what he knows about himself, including the mirroring and roles given to him by his society.

Mind uses complex 'time/change maps' called images: archaic, useful, the organised sounds of language gradually coming to evoke them in later evolution. You have a glimpse of a friend further down the shopping mall. Sometimes you are wrong; it is a stranger.

The representation in Mind is of an image drawing its form from sensory input, memory, context and an aspect of Mind making constructs of the immediately expected future.

It works best with a clear head in daylight.

Yet perception may change abruptly: the stick may become a snake or the snake a stick as the right foot is poised in the air.

Like a fluorescent screen the image persists to four dimensions, and fills in the likely immediate future too, as George Kelly discerned. And yet while Mind is everything, there are the aspects of Mind to be tested: like skin against orange-tree bark and the air entering the nose.

In Mind there is the illusion they are there in four dimensions, together with many other aspects from the senses, such as the odour, the sensory input from tendon and joint, let alone the mood/feeling, sense of quality evoked.

What is there, is the sequential impingement of elaborate processes: what

Development VI

is experienced is an aromatic tree with green leaves and the promise of fruit. The dimensions are needed for the highly useful illusions, in the form of multidimensional maps when the consistency of Mind is being sought.

As the orange tree is in flower, the fragrance - fifth dimension, is evoking the other four. Mind is an orange tree.

By scientific method, Mind can be highly consistent in the macroscopic world, and even the particle world's inconsistency has consistent principles.

So the movement/image that is 'bus' might be caught to Bondi, or perceived receding up the hill. And that is no different from fingers, thumb and pen as they write. Mind maps them: back, buttock, bus seat: totally one — four dimensional Mind.

It is very different to the non-living surface of Mars being itself without an observer. There: 'now' is 'now' is 'now', and so it is here, but it does not seem to be. The system juxtaposes images and information, whether from perception or memory, into Now. And if not cluttered with too many words, or 'I-focussed' thoughts, they are there together.

For Mind to be even a useful illusion, this juxtaposition together of elements of happening is vital. They are connected by the image stabilising properties of the nervous system, despite their origins before or after each other of however many milliseconds.

And how the processor can do it! The student has difficulty with enlightenment because he or she is not prepared for the utter immensity of Now. They confuse it with small 'n' now and the illusory objective 'now'.

They underestimate the ability of the nervous system. It can juxtapose not only all its senses, but memory, images and anticipation to form intricate multi- dimensional maps, and, as well, neurophysiological systems can overview all of this, selecting aspects for close attention.

This overview is vividly apparent during zazen. The intuitive overviewing function is enhanced when the static and confusion is quietened and the setting has lost 'this' and 'that' dimensions. It can be further developed.

How wonderful the illusion of holding 'a thick film of now' when one thought seems to merge with the next, the vivid memories of the last ten seconds, and the nervous system that can play Grieg to itself with some illusion of an orchestra, and avoid being run down in Woolworth's carpark. How adaptive?

This processor has had this capacity long before it evolved the illusion of 'I' with a verbal label.

How extraordinary is 'The always so' to have developed the illusion of knowing aspects of Itself. How innovative to explore 'Its' consistencies.

Yet if one thinks about the survival of organisms whose every function is movement/change 'now', to thus survive, the organism must be able to adapt to adverse change: The reflex to drop a hot fire-iron is useful, but avoiding a collision is another matter, and reading a weather-map something more.

These are Now/Reality/ Suchness, as is anything else, just as Pirsig knew the essential oneness of the function of a motor-cycle engine and the aesthetic appreciation of a landscape.

CHANGE

When one organised parcel of changes — an organism — renews to adapt to change, inherent is Universal Self. Change itself would be the character of such a creature.

Reproduction, differentiation into myriad species, competition, social support and conflict: change itself becomes adaptive, is highly flexible in coping with other changes. The illusion of time: anticipation, the process of judgement: is more necessary for the sequence of changes that are survival for a species.

So, necessarily, the nervous system itself is change of a rapid and complex order, change that can outstrip many other changes. Call it 'superchange' or 'ultrachange' or something like that. But when tested by an earthquake or a fast bowler, it has its limitations.

The organism has become very complex; complex enough to fool itself, and fool itself adaptively, yet rarely complex enough to know itself. This is why we sit to experience Now/Dhyana, how we find simplicity and emptiness. We retreat from illusion to Reality.

Zazen is a total experience of what is 'seen', and as kensho brings the next view and then the next (because this is the experience), it will all be zazen. It then pervades even the emotionally charged interactions with others. It becomes Self-accelerated development: the source of 'Heart' that Ms Schloegl indicates so well.

The contrary is also true. The illusory aspects of functioning, such as memory and anticipation and imagination, allow us to fully avail ourselves of processes to argue, to develop, to socialise and to organise, and even to communicate by speech and writing. The illusions are adaptive. Adaptive illusions bring about development. What a wonderful, wonderful 'Always so'.

And the organism resonating with the movement/change, being a 'sound' within a 'sound' at non-existent 'now', juxtaposes all that 'neuronal sound' to the illusion of 'form', and the illusion of 'time' allows the illusion of 'something'.

Small 'r' reality thinks, and gives birth to Reality.

"The barking of the two-legged dog."

Sunyatta, that Sanskrit word difficult to translate, thus needs a physicist and not a philosopher. It is misleading to those who rely on language to translate it as 'void', or 'nothing'. 'Emptiness' is better, 'no thing' is certainly less misleading; the Chinese "Wu" is perhaps something more.

Physicists are learning philosophy, and philosophers are learning physics - imagine the development in that.

Yet some scientists looking at the nature of the cosmos, when attracted to the parallel conclusions of physics and what they call Eastern Mysticism, seek a quality of inexplicable magic in meditation that allows great leaps of insight.

They talk as if neuroscience, although much more in its infancy than their own, is still open to magic transformation in the areas where there are great gaps in our knowledge.

There is a duality in this: a belief that a hypothesis arrived at by an intuitive overview, might be from a different Universe than one that can be tested by quantitative measurement.

Yet scientists are adept at putting aside verbal thinking, and summarise their own intuition by diagrams or mathematical expressions: "Knowing is like this: it is all of it there in the Now", as she marks out a diagrammatic schema on the nearest piece of paper.

The problem arises because the nervous system functions by the integration of multiple systems in parallel. A new generation of computers is being developed to imitate this neurophysiological capacity. In contrast, words appear on the page, or are spoken one at a time. Explanations in words are limited by this sequential function of language. This difficulty is in translating a complex picture into a linear one or vice-versa.

Overviews are perceived as a gestalt arrived at intuitively, and are represented in the nervous systems in images, maps, or integrates of more than one system — they are shifting juxtapositions seen as a dynamic whole do not allow of easy explanation.

All this means is that your brain can do moving pictures, put up a number of images together, connect them with a sense of their dynamic movement in various circumstances: how do you tell of it all in words?

That it is not readily explicable might make it 'mystic' in the philosophic meaning of the word, but a natural process nonetheless.

Development VI

While physicists marvel at the ancient sage's correct conclusions, they might better marvel at those conclusions being formed by making the most of what little data was available. Although data arrived at through the experience of meditation is not the physicist's apple, we are more likely to have them sampling it when they do not throw up their hands and cry mystification, but rather see it as another aspect of 'complementarity': the 'uncertain' tested for consistency.

Zen seeks to bring a simple view of the world of matter/energy stripped of the clutter of a culture's beliefs, and relieved of the surmise of magic.

Strip the word 'mystic' of any connotations of 'secret', 'transcendental', 'enigmatic', or 'psychic' or other evocations to do with difficult notions, ancient knowledge and the experience of Saints, and there is little left for most people.

Better is the philosophic meaning referring to insight not being explicable in words. It might be limited to the connotation of one who is awake to the nature of the Universe and would apply to a wide variety of men and women.

But surely 'mystic' is a confusing word in view of its other usages.
If there are secrets let us expose them here.

The inevitable koan

There are many who are interested in Zen, but angry that an explanation seems hidden, or, expressed in a manner that they find confusing. It is regrettable and sad that it is not easier.

For it to be available to more men and women would be most desirable. It is important that their curiosity is aroused and they are not made to feel put-down by what is a different task to those at which they have been successful.

So, were a theologian to question, what could be said about this view of Zen Buddhism? The response would be mostly about feeling. The words might be some- thing like: "Self is recognised — only Self."

And the 'seeing'/zazen? What was intuitively recognised that Friday?

Making a list of required elements distorts the view, rather than reflecting 'The Sound', as a series of still photographs would be unable to reflect a vibrant ballerina's solo.

> In considering whether to write this section at all, was the unacceptance of mysticism as discussed elsewhere. Indeed, the author wants to demonstrate that 'Zen' is illogical for the reason that language is limited and distracting, but Zen is nevertheless rational, in that language is only one of many tools to express data, hypothesis and theory essential to the sharing of Scientific Method.

There is no requirement that rationality be confined to what may be expressed in language. It would be a denial of the parallel processing capacity of the neuronal net to so confine it, and destroy the value of diagram, image, graph, and evocation of feeling by art, as well as the zen method of transmitted intuition.

So, writing in this vein is a break from zen tradition. This tradition arose because the masters were aware that 'seeing' was not expressible in words, and that words confused and distracted from the essence, indeed were a destructive element to their pupil's development, and often trapped him or her in egocentric preoccupation. However, this writing is presented to give the analytic some idea of the difficulties.

'The analytic': those who would look at the smaller systems, and then try to understand the larger from 'the bottom up'. They have been well served by inductive logic, the convergence of knowing all the elements to find the true whole: this includes numerous people who might feel turned away from Zen. Let us give them an opportunity too.

Development VI

Also in trouble is the tenet of those who believe the English language's capacity to express anything. Hence the pivotal importance of the quote about 'experience' from Paul Tillich in 'God is a verb'.

To validly reflect development at VI, the elements below do not consider those kensho already described, which have been minimised, not integrated, or inchoate aspects that are not yet seen clearly (or at all).

Let us just bring together expressions already used and say it is a wholeness and consistency of these:

> **'Not I' ('The Sound', Self)**
> **'Just this' (Mind/Now/Reality)**
> **'All this' moves as it moves and is testable**
> **No boundary (in any dimension) — Utter Oneness**
> **Timelessness**
> **and Heart (acquires its capital 'H')**

(But each of these elements may have taken years of work to see clearly, and rendering 'The Sound' in this manner is artificial, 'bitty', and misleading, as each one can stand for the other, and looking at the six lines, they look like a stack of bricks. They are more different points of view, than elements to aggregate. They are loose, flexible: start anywhere, go anyway; the ten Developments themselves are only traditional division of development/no development)

Also, there are the two special viewpoints (modes) of 'seeing' this as a whole:

> **'Mu'**
> **and 'Bodhisattva action'.**

Expressed as a diagram whose purpose is to convey aspects of unity and to evoke movement, this orbital ellipse might be revealing, however even the word 'modes' is misleading because they are not separate and two, but 'Utterly One'.

The difficulty is that each element on the diagram is itself inexplicable, being the result of 'experience', and then the realisation of kensho.

So, the words in and around the elliptic orbit have meaning to those who have done much hard work. The origin of this difficulty was discussed earlier in 'The barking of the two-legged dog.'

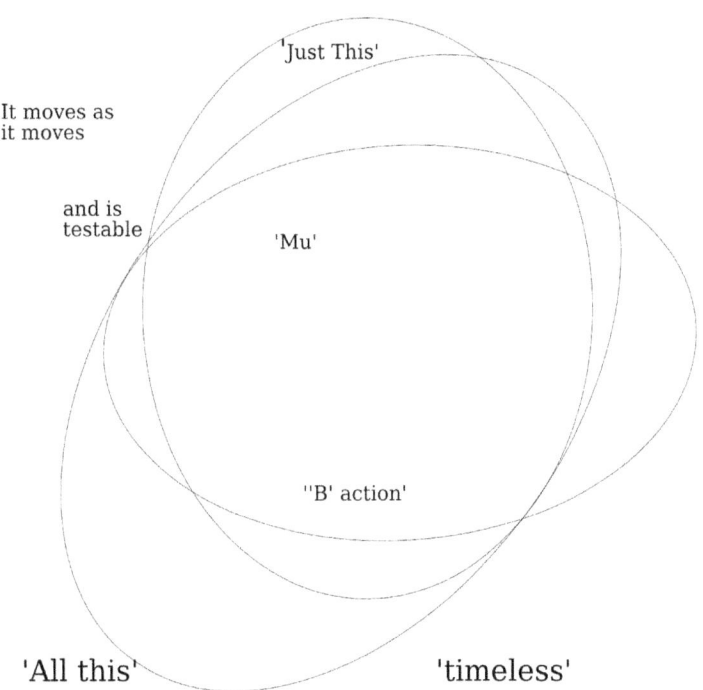

'B' action' = Bodisattva action

Development VI

Let us look at these views:

'All this' moves as It moves, and is testable. This is science and its methods; it is also the pain in the back, food and drink, and the "now" of an automobile collision. In earlier experience it was the hand striking the wall, and the story of the monastery gate.

'No boundaries' — in any dimension. Remember the story of the small aeroplane in the storm.

'Not I' is the house without its ridge-pole, but what is there when 'I' is not? It is meditation, it is how everything/ nothing is — Now/Mind/Reality. But put a tree in 'Now', or the morning star.

Heart — the feeling intimately owned when 'I' is let off the bus.

Timelessness is the easiest one to approach by Western thought about the nature of the Universe, including some physics and neuroscience: time is a dimension of measurement that distracts until it is seen like any other dimension.

The measure and measurer are inseparable: the vector required for the measurer to function creates the illusion of the measure.

Utter Oneness This is a view: both common-sense and philosophical: where there is no duality whatsoever

Illusion certainly distracts from the two 'modes' of seeing.

First: 'Mu', the Japanese translation of the Chinese 'Wu': 'nothing', 'emptiness', 'the void'. When asked did a dog have Buddha nature, Joshu (Chao-Chou 778-897 AD) made a noise "Wu" that he really meant in every respect.

When it seems that Buddhism seems to extol the 'void' many are put off or discouraged; they imagine emptiness and nothing Playing in the surf: a wave knocks you off your feet.

It is examined further in 'Buddhism as a Philosophy' on p164.
Yet a concrete thinker might reject it with contempt.

Look at Dogen's view of Hui-Nêng's bell (late Twentieth Century version): the metal vibrates, the air, the eardrum and cochlear hairs, the eighth   cranial nerve does its complex depolarisations, the neuro-transmitters move across the synapses to their receptors, the auditory cortex depolarises in its patterns, order supervenes, a visual representation of the bell might make re-entry in partnership between the cortex and cerebellar vermis: the visualised bell may not be a good representation compared with the one that might have been seen by the eyes.

And all this movement/change in the air, the brain, not to mention the bell? What is it?

It is exactly this 'process, nothing' aspect of Buddhism that is hard for many to grasp. That Quality/energy is only such when represented in Mind, is one point. That this is the sum effect of virtual processes which interact with the nervous system to produce it, is another. And when a Scientific theory is formulated, it too is about process.

Mu' from its 'doggyness', sound and action, is a koan with no apparent teaching but it incorporates 'Just this, Utter Oneness and when really experienced - transcendental emptiness: nirvana.

Mu' is truly about the nature of self in all its levels, truth, unity and nirvana, and just as true when the action mode of enlightenment is in full activity. Put another way: True emptiness transcends, but from emptiness comes all the energy for action.

Yet the experience of 'Mu' is indescribable in language. To say what it is not, might be attempted. But to communicate to somebody else who knows, is like communicating across a crowded room to one's cousin, when Grandfather retells one of his favoured stories.

The other special view of enlightenment is through 'Bodhisattva action'. 'Not I' acts to prevent suffering, to preserve, succour and develop its creatures, to see Itself more clearly. The Unborn is utterly involved with Its own development.

> *Yet development in this aspect of 'sight' is still rudimentary, and so also is fitting it into the wider picture.*

Development VI

WITHOUT VISION OF GOOSE OR BOTTLE

The required factors for the kensho described at the end of Development V are set out here.

The experience is that this kensho is only one of many on the way, and it develops further from there. This one was only different in that it was a linking of others into one frame. It is also likely that it came suddenly this way because there was no teacher to reflect the essence. and kensho was long overdue, thus comprehensive development was missed and intimate sight with a good teacher.

When the sitting becomes zazen, there is a developing appreciation of Just This. The nature of Just This as process/change is comprehended unequivocally. The seeming paradox between 'complexity' and 'nothing' is resolved. Zazen and 'seeing' are realised as One and turning back is impossible.

The smallness of what 'Not I' can perceive of itself in Just This might be crushing, but All This and Just This cannot differ. Mind/Now / Reality is meaningful and 'Not I' is accepted.

The daily experience of 'All This' is complex, undisciplined and distracting. But experiment to test 'All This' can be undertaken, and the aspects of the natural Universe are enormous, so All This is as it is ('moves as it moves' or 'processes as it processes' is less illusory), and is testable. In the method to assess its consistency and inconsistency, to make predictions, is Science.

If together with this, The Goose is truly 'out' and there is no boundary in any of the dimensions, the meaning of "and there is nothing else" will be understood.

For all these elements, the development is relatively early and this section **rightly in the middle of the book**. At the end its is necessary for more before beginning work as a journeyman.

Of 'movement' and all its synonyms: 'time' is an illusion inherent in relative motion, and 'Something' is an illusion inherent in relative motion too: relatively slower motion particularly, and in 'the collapse of the wave function' that comes from the measuring stick and the organism who wields it, as well as its statistical effects resonating in that organism.

In some circumstances wave function impinges on the neuronal net where it then processes as 'Something'. Putting this last bit another way, the nerve cell net resonates in its own time scale, in its own fashion, **with only some processes of 'The Sound'**, and then only to large aggregates of process to which the net's photographic plate' will respond.

Think of the deaf, or the colour blind; they perceive differently. And X. rays, for example, are only detectable if a fluorescent screen or a film is exposed to them and this is visually examined. Some of these have proved fresh and valuable over centuries: such koan are the vitality of zen.

> *The experiment in such communication inevitably becomes pages of koan-like writing. To plead that what must be known clearly within the receiver's nervous system, must be genuine and first hand: is that an excuse for the inadequacy of these words for the learned reader, words that will be felt by the earnest student as obscure? Are koan a hostile put-down for the uninitiated? Are they playthings or teaching tools? Could there be better ones? Or perhaps intermediate ones that would allow quicker transition to the important ones?*
>
> *Yet "seeing cannot be explained. It is of a different order than most stimulating words, yet taking 'seeing' to words in a pithy drama, sometimes produces paradoxes which could be a lead-in to intuitive awareness.*

In living that meaning however, it is necessary to go past koan. Being 'out' in the goose's sense, must be 'out' without visions of goose and bottle. And 'seeing' will be 'seeing' in a complex social interchange, just as seeing is "seeing zazen."

Development VI

'ARROW, STICK OR HINT?'

The difficulty for one treading 'the way' is with the verbal expressions that sweep across the whole. They clearly mean something to those who demonstrate or dissertate about them

From those who have some 'sight', they are meant as arrow, stick, or hint anyway, a stimulus to those who would 'see'.

Examples are, "Not I' and 'The sound of one hand clapping' They express This, which is utterly one. This includes greed, kindness, magpies, envy, muffins, charity, catacombs, famine, insight, cruelty, leptons, war, cats, love, nurture, deliverance, vegemite sandwiches, vodka, baseball, quasars and the residents of Popov St: an essential truth expressed in a distinct style in the Bhagavad Gita.

The 'seeing' of some elements is a way to 'seeing' the others, but 'seeing' is an unhesitating appreciation of the nature of self that is Self.

It might be easier however, when you know there are many words, koan or expressions that mean essentially the same to the user, but if the intention is to prod understanding in one direction or to illustrate a special quality of 'The always so', then a particular Name is chosen.

Coming from another direction or to give a fresh point of view, a different name might be better. The Absolute Self was used by Suzuki and The Unborn by Shakyamuni. But it might be just personal choice. The author uses The Sound because that's the way it happened.

2022 author
.... after the colossal creativity experience floods the view — 'Herself'.

So, in 'seeing', there is an understanding of why Absolute Self, Action, Buddha-nature, Now, Dhyana (zazen and zen), The Goose, Heart, Mind, This, Reality, Eternity Now, Emptiness, Tao, Impermanence, Change, Self, The Universal Self, The Eternal Face, It, The Unborn, The Utterly One, Quality/energy, "The always so, 'Wu'! (or Mu!), Dharma, Sunyatta, 'suchness' and 'the sound of one hand clapping are metaphor for facets of The Sound: shadows of what is 'seen'. And these are only some of them.

*A good teacher would have helped with the goose noises and the "**t**" sound at the "end" of 'The goose is out', and then, instead of talking about The Sound, it might have been The Goose.*

Fear of Seeing

Certainly, the major impediment to being 'awake' is the difficulty in giving up views and beliefs already held, and held by the culture around, and indeed inherent in the language. To this must be added the strength to bear the truth and all its implications, and the simple fear of 'seeing'.

Beneath that fear is the underlying fear that was first coped with in childhood by dividing the world into 'goods' and 'baddies': better the 'B'-grade Hollywood movie, with a clear division into 'goodies' and 'baddies' than the unconnected and unpredictable bits of self for various circumstances.

Beyond that division is the trust to bear 'good' and 'bad' (quality) together. Elliott Jacques (a Kleinian) saw accepting their integration universally as the zenith of maturation. While this is inherent in zen development too, it is far from all of it.

Jung called his version of a sound self 'individuation' because it must ultimately occur in each nervous system, and the French psychoanalyst Jacques Lacan likened development to stripping the layers from an onion. Who or what would be left? When 'I' only is identified with the outer layers of the onion, enlightenment is a death.

There are hopes from the wish fulfilment phases of childhood that would be dashed by enlightenment. There is fear at giving them up.

But experiencing what remains is ordinary 'everyday'. Still this prospect is frightening to many, and the result appears 'mystic' to others.

Development VI

'I': ADAPTIVE ILLUSION AND MALIGN TEMPTATION.

On Christmas Eve, 'Not I' snows and blows, walks and chats. Yet even the expression 'Not I' is about process, not a 'something'. And self too is process: 'selfing' if you like, highly integrated: seeing, feeling, thinking, doing. The illusion is immediate: multi-dimensional and alive. Wonderful!

Whatever the need for the illusion however, when skipping, it would seem strange to respond to the question "Who are you?" with "Skip.

In contrast to self, 'I' is a collection of garnered beliefs about a 'somebody', whether about worth, status or capacity. Snowflakes blow against your lips, 'I, the beliefs, and the neural schemata behind 'I': two orders of process removed from such impacts.

Why does T' seem so consequential to many cultures?

Self- preserving responses of any organism is some of it; leadership, role and status in the community, and originality for diverse development is more.

In childhood particularly, the focus of attention on the individual is intensely important for nurture and protection: and to provide security of attachment.

From the natural 'not I' position of the skink, the young child needs to know their individual body is not a magic extension of their parent, that it will be hurt, needs to make its own moves to avoid the problems of reality, then be able to turn back to parents from a unique and whole position. It is not always easy to do this.

Some are still struggling against parent images; others stay adhered to them. Different societies have different ways of looking at 'I' and thus experiencing 'I. Why do some take the position of a defensive 'I' within 'the skin and clothing fortress'? Why does this seem more necessary in one culture than another?

Essentially the child runs the gauntlet of his or her culture; now the growing global culture. There are unreachable examples on every screen. The child may be humiliated or rejected, feel that 'I' will never be good enough for parents or fit those images.

Confusing prescriptions for living are everywhere. Some need impenetrable defenses. 'I' is subject to shame and guilt. 'I' must accept consumer gratification and seek status with peers. There are many clichés for this treadmill and many attempts to avoid it by lifestyle or location.

The paradox is that individuation and maturity develop by appropriate social boundary and autonomy of thought, not by acquiring 'I' prescriptions from others.

This can be confronted within.

Further there are situations where 'I' is more than defensive, the skin is replaced with psychic armour: the gratifications of 'I' become the 'rewards' of giving up awareness of bodhi.

Hence the parable of Faust: who, surrendered, whatever else, his connection with God for the primary temptation — gratification of the wishes of 'I'.

Faust had the ultimate want of the person who is aware in some way that 'I' is dynamic rather than static, and hence transitory. It is significant that Shakyamuni and Jesus were both tempted in this manner before their ministries.

Faust was wanting the 'I' to be more than virtual, wanting the gratifications without the inevitable loss and dissatisfaction : that is Faust's essential requirement.

Here is the origin of suffering. It is brought home to some when billionaires have a heart attack or kings develop cancer.

When Shakyamuni saw the morning star and Jesus returned from the wilderness their understanding of this issue was true.

If Interested in Jesus

The experience of Jesus was also immediately different.

Discussing Jesus makes some interested, and others want to turn away: it gives them strong feelings, particularly related to their experience of those who preached to them, judged them, rejected them, or even bored them with Jesus.

With some 'sight' a Zen Buddhist 'sees' his identity with Hui- Nêng, Chao-Chua (Joshu) and Dogen, as well as Shakyamuni:

So, it is not an extraordinary utterance to say to those interested, "Jesus lives": The Sermon on the Mount; "The Kingdom of God is within you."; loving neighbour as self; 'as a young child'; cutting across social mores; 'the body and the blood': the honour of women; 'the other cheek' and the problems of the rich man.

For those Christians who are interested in zazen practice, they might also try "You must become as a little child to enter the Kingdom of Heaven" as a first koan (see also pages 39 to 40), and when this is exhaustively part of you, "*Before Abraham was, I am*": — then, "*This is my body, this is my blood*", itself. Here is Teilhard's concept of The Christic.

Faith is not required. But, a warning — this is of Jesus, not the structures of Christianity.

The confused scribe?

In some versions of the Buddha's life, Shakyamuni worked as many miracles as the Indian imagination could devise.

Brahma's presence is acknowledged in the Sutras, even if less emphasised than the content of Shakyamuni's enlightenment.

There is a point where the original writing about Shakyamuni and Jesus must reflect the understanding his master's experience and message. But he will only do as well as his own and his culture's belief systems, and if he did not understand, translation is a problem, or written communication is not suited to the material, then there is confusion for those who follow.

Muhammed personally committed his revelation to writing. Jesus' experience of The Cross and graphic expression overcame much of the difficulty, but others told stories about both Jesus and Shakyamuni that sought to give them credibility by asking us to accept the working of miracles.

Shakyamuni's attitude to miracles is unambiguous in his response to the householder of Nalanda, when he stated his shame at supernatural miracles, said he disliked the mind-reading miracle, whereas living the Brahma-life was a miracle he respected, saying this would provide the necessary strength to resist any power.

There is no doubt of his humour too. When he met the ascetic yogi who had been trying to walk across the surface of the river for some decades, he advised him to go across with the aid of a small coin given to the ferryman.

Development VI

'The Sound'

This view of 'miracles' was from a fresh direction. It was if those that sought them looked for action 'outside' 'the sound of one hand'. In looking outside, wanting more, they were looking for a process or a Somebody, separate, permanent, and essentially dual. They were seeking in the wrong direction.

Perhaps they must accept and then grieve that they cannot impose inconsistency and discontinuity — wishful duality upon 'The always so', before the search can begin.

In contrast, hope is quite different to wishing and wanting: the virtual outcome is held in intuition Now.

A hope: For he or she to look into self and 'see The Sound and know It is wonder indeed.

> To face in that direction?
>
> *Development VI is a contrast to the quiet practice of Zen. There is no outward behaviour corresponding to these writings. The many aspects of The Sound are not spouted enthusiastically.*
>
> *Zen is not about excited transformation or preoccupation with the Godhead. It would be too easy for development to be distracted, or become intellectual, suggestible and second-hand as a result of such a show.*
>
> *Each has a right to his or her first-hand Development.*
>
> *'Nevertheless, this is an attempt at an authentic reflection of how it happened in 1987.'*
>
> **"Talk of the Buddha and wash out your mouth."**

JESUS ENLIGHTENED?

Reading The New Testament, we are reliant on the insight of the early writers, and confused by esoteric meanings of some expressions where symbolic language was used.

This leaves a Buddhist with an important question. Especially a Buddhist with strong bonds to Christianity. That is, 'Was Jesus enlightened?'

The writers of the gospels so steep their account in their own beliefs, there is evidence denying enlightenment and evidence supporting it.

If enlightened, there is the problem of the scribes not understanding this enlightenment yet positive evidence comes from various sources.

Jesus saw neighbour as self. Tellingly he indicated that the hungry, the thirsty, the sick and the naked, the stranger and those in prison, were as himself, and however they were treated it was as if to himself.

The story of being tempted by "The Devil' in the wilderness is clearly an appeal to 'I' to experience desire and seek its gratification aggrandisement, further elaboration of 'I' power, with riches.

The purification of rejecting this is total. If more was known of the development required to resist the temptations of 'I', then surely Christianity would more resemble Buddhism. This whole consistent teaching, is it experience of timeless Unity, or First Century supernaturalism, or is it ritualised language of the Essenes?

The radical compassionate ethics arising from the Christian dharma is the best indication.

On the other hand, how would the scribes express it? We know it was an age of intense spiritual preoccupation. The extant culture would have required prophetic, theistic and sacrificial elements, and each writing would have met the needs of the people from whose context it was written.

Nevertheless, essential elements of the enlightenment would have survived along with inevitable conclusions.

Some of these are pivotal to the essence of Christianity, such as the warnings about projection: the mote in the other's eye, the dangerous outcome from these, and of the destructiveness of 'bad other' preoccupations.

Christians who understand this at depth spread good outcome about them. Because the teachings on this issue in the Gospel are so frank and unambiguous, those Christians who do not put these into their living behaviour are easily discounted, but the point missed here, is that the words alone won't do it: they require insight before incorporating 'Right Action' into day to day living.

A short book called 'Zen and the Bible' by the enlightened Jesuit, Father J.K. Kadowaki, is to be recommended here.

While the question of the nature of Jesus' enlightenment remains, the teaching about behaviour is clear. However, some, usually without realising it, fall into the way of worshipping 'the book' itself. There seems to be a distraction from contemplation of the great themes of The New Testament.

This difference in emphasis between Christianity and Buddhism that is larger than might have otherwise been. This is amplified by the perception that Buddhism is about withdrawal rather than engagement: inward looking rather than involved, recommending personal development rather than its value to others.

Shakyamuni's view of the futility and hollowness of seeking for power, riches or aggrandisement may provide some of this confusion. It may also be interpreted as passivity and misunderstood by those who focus on the words used to express the Buddhist experience.

While not as pivotal as Jesus' enlightenment, the effects of early Christianity and Buddhism upon one another are still under study, and interest has been aroused.

Were Christians in India at the end of the First Century A.D. influencing Nagarjuna and the Buddhist Council who brought about the early beginning of Mahayana, with emphasis upon the enlightened Bodhisattva saving others and creating good outcome for many creatures?

The great Buddhist Emperor of India, Ashoka (Third Century BC), sent missionaries in all directions including Alexandria and Greece. They were established in at least the former. Holger Kersten points out that Jesus' style of mission, although three hundred years later, was much more like that of the Buddhist monks than the style of Judea at that time.

However, The Gospel is the most indicative. While Shakyamuni's line of blind men leading each other could be coincidence, the use of the tale about the poor widow's contribution of two small coins by the author of The Gospel According to St Mark cannot be coincidence in every detail. (Mark 12: 41-44)

It is difficult to know whether Sutra or Gospel borrowed this story from the other because of its inherent value or whether Jesus re-enacted it.

All we know however, is that the two major religions were not in separate worlds. In the intervening half millennium, the silk road was active, the Persians and Macedonians had political power in both worlds, and there was massive migration as Semitic peoples were taken East into servitude.

For those who are curious, Holger Kersten puts forward material and references about parallels between Gospel and Sutra, as well as comparative religious development and monastic life. It is an important area for further research, and for the scholarly determinations to be checked and corroborated.

> Zen Buddhism puts aside 'the book', because it is a distraction to 'seeing'. Zen Buddhist tradition is of a teaching without words directed at knowing the nature of self and becoming 'awake. Each is sent off to his or her 'wilderness to know the nature of his or her self. "Seeing is an outgrowth of this experience. The Buddhist identity is with the processes of 'Not I'. It is utterly One.

The Gnostics

Gnosis is Greek for 'knowing'. We are told that the Gnostic Christians of Egypt and Rome in the Second and Third Century AD, saw the world, particularly matter, as imperfect, the product of an inept creator, and kept in that manner by archons, the fallen emissaries of this creator.

By knowing 'The One True Spirit' and becoming one with 'The Father', they were born again finding the Kingdom of Heaven, regaining their own original spirit. The knowing was transmitted by teacher to disciple when the latter was ready 'like a mirror'. The beliefs were variable, dualistic and not humble.

Valentinus (Second Century AD) of Alexandria was said to be the founder of this movement, although gnostic ideas had undoubtedly been extant earlier and may have been derived from the monastic Therapeutae and Essenes. Each was to find his own gnosis.

The Gnostic movement was unpopular with The Church, and the Nicene creed was in reaction to the movement. It was formally made a heresy in the late Third or early Fourth Century AD. It may be coincidental that it was around this time the books of the Nag Hammadi library were buried in their sealed pot, whether with an interment, or the hiding of non-acceptable material, are open to conjecture.

However, all works of this library were works not included in the present day Bible. Most importantly, it contained a manuscript of The Gospel According to Thomas. A second manuscript of this gospel has been found since.

The crisis for Christianity was between the Gnostics and those who were to be saved by Baptism and Faith, hopefully to hold to Jesus' clear teaching how to behave in the world, but who did not 'know'. The latter prevailed, but belief was resurrectionist, concrete and codified. However, reincarnation beliefs were not proscribed until much later.

The important question: did Gnostic beliefs arise from simpler enlightened beliefs held over a century earlier?

And had that earlier gnosis the opportunity to meet 'Reality in prayer, become aware of the oneness of 'inside and outside' thus utter Oneness, and the nature of form? Were there Alexandrian Buddhists or spiritual Therapeutae with enlightened views, who influenced First Century religious thought?

What did 'The Father', 'The Kingdom of Heaven', and 'The One True Spirit'

refer to in this earlier knowing?
If it was a direct experience, as samadhi experience of Oneness is to a Buddhist, it is intuited and not easy to communicate.

(Jesus said): *If asked for a sign of your Father,
answer: "Movement and Repose."*

The Gospel according to Thomas 50, 5 - 9.

When a Buddhist talks of being 'unborn' and 'deathless', rises from zazen as Now, is this similar to that other quote from 'The Gospel according to Thomas' where Jesus says in response to the disciples' question about their own end.

*Have you already discovered
The Beginning, now that
You are asking about the end?
Wherever the Beginning is,
there shall be the end.
Blessed is he who stands
At the Beginning, for he understands
The end without tasting death.*

The Gospel according to Thomas 18, 4-11

In the canonical gospels, Jesus not only talks of 'being as a little child' being necessary to enter the Kingdom of Heaven, he talks about smallness and humility. What could better describe the experience at the brink of 'seeing'? But it is like a mustard seed, he says. From its smallness it might grow.

Brahma

There are quite a few difficulties when people want particular qualities to God. Some want a Him. They want a supernatural being; and if there are many supernatural beings, then the good one needs to be the strongest and the most caring. They want this Being to intervene in day-to-day affairs. At the deepest level they want to be made in His image.

The big difficulty to a Buddhist is when God is required to be 'a something — a Somebody!' There are those who want the dancer rather than the dance.

Teilhard understood the process aspect of everything: movement, everything changes, and that it was going on to change further, including humanity — even God would evolve, Teilhard said. But Teilhard was much more centered on Jesus than God. The Christic fills Teilhard's evolution.

Like Teilhard, Küng faces Unity. He wants God uncontaminated by shamanistic magic. If the kind, protective actions of humanity are viewed as an aspect of Immanence in all matter/ energy, and not the work of a Deity transcendent in separateness, then Kung's Brahma will accommodate to the next cycle of spiritual awareness.

Vidal would be unlikely to accept this. But The One God, preferably in man's image, is important to mankind in so many ways. He or She is One: not many. He or She can be a receptacle for the ideal, as well as the liege, the powerful one, so that this role is not invested in a human. Or the elements of The One Deity may be humanised as in Jesus made within reach.

Historically, a common form is essentially a fragmentation of the deity, many gods such as those of the Greeks and Romans, the Gods being humanised with strengths and weaknesses. In Western society this element is readily translated into the plots of mainstream soap operas to satisfy those who require it.

To contain the fears and insecurity of those whose world would be plagued by evil forces, the God who can control the others is essential.

Particularly when the deity is broken up into Lords of the Underworld, creators of evil, Satan, Kali — it is most important that one God is supreme.

Even more chaotic is the world of spirits, malign and capricious, their appeasement a basic need in a highly insecure existence.

The intelligent becomes shaman, a go-between with the frightening and the powerful.

The One God is the salvation of man from this abyss. Vidal, in his critique of the confusion and groveling before such a God, has lost his memory of being at the mercy of the supernatural. From that position of development, security lies in praising The Lord and knowing unambiguously what The Lord requires of you.

Küng is aware that a Buddhist has his or her equivalent of The Absolute even if 'The Utterly One' is totally dynamic. But the validity of this lies in the dynamic complexity of process: the essence of change/development that begets loving, knowledge, health and wonder. With our eyes in this direction, Kung's 'Unnamed God of the Buddhists' is not pantheistic as a Something/ Somebody, or a 'God of Matter', but The Dynamic Suchness of All.

Development VI

"GOD IS A VERB."

So, from a Buddhist point of view, if aspects of the dharma such as the loving of people for one another, the joy in the process of work, the occurrence of fine weather in a good land, the growing of fruit on the tree are manifestations of 'God' the process that is Utterly One: then believing in 'God' or not believing in 'God' is a matter of semantics.

Thus, God is 'love' in the doing, changing things, happening sense, rather than God is Love the concept, or 'love the sentiment': 'loving' is the real thing.

'God' to a Buddhist would always be a verb and never a noun, and would be an inappropriate word to describe the wondrous process a Buddhist experiences, and the compassionate action he is able to take.

When Shakyamuni stood from sitting beneath the pipal tree and saw the morning star, he initially thought that what he 'saw was too subtle or too difficult to teach. But it was this Brahma aspect that led to his loving communication of his 'sight' to all who wanted it.

Yet this is not God 'The First Cause', or Creator, it is not Providence intervening supernaturally in day-to-day affairs. This is not a separate being revealing himself to the privileged, or dividing humanity into two or three classes to be accepted for Heaven or to be rejected to damnation or purgation.

The United States theologian Tillich, when considering the history of religions, recognised that a theology not "rooted in its experiential basis" is not possible. What of the experience of intrinsic ethics?

What of the experience of need for a leader and a closeness to him? "How can a Buddhist bear being without the powerful loving presence of Jesus beside him?" a Christian might ask. The Buddhist might smile, reply that it was more difficult being unenlightened, but there is The Buddha, The Dharma and The Sangha — called The Three Treasures. And Jesus? Why not Jesus there too?

To a Buddhist with some 'sight' there are two ways of experiencing the truth of this: Jesus beside him sure: but being beside 'Jesus': sandals on dusty tracks, the smell of donkeys and blood, the horror of iron nails and total helplessness, nevertheless 'Union with the Father'.

'Seeing' does not stop there: the driver of the nails, every abused child and the conscripts and generals of a thousand armies — all One.

Development VI

And the koan quoted by Father Kadowaki: 'National Teacher Daito's comment on the koan *'Joshu sees through an old woman': which is "All say he carries a lamp to light his way in broad daylight, they don't know he has lost his money and is charged with the crime as well."*: another legendary piece about Joshu (Chao- Chua).

Buddhists who see themselves in a different Universe to Christians might need be cautious about this koan in the gut. What did Joshu live for? But a Buddhist as theist, is so in only the broadest sense. Call him or her a 'dharmist', or some other new word if that is easier.

In the Hindu absorption of Buddhism following the suppression of Buddhism after the Islamic conquests, 'The All' has developed as Brahman, taking the form of gods, goddesses, men and women, the individual soul Atman playing a part, not realising The Absolute is the real actor. Shakyamuni saw that Atman is Universal Self .. full stop: that the notion of a distinct and separate Atman reborn to fur or feather, scale or caste was dualist and flawed.

But Brahman is Oneness / Everything. The belief is written out, rather than known', but would seem to owe as much to Buddhism as to the supreme Vedic deity of the early Aryan invaders.

While it is easy to see the lifelong curiosity and struggle around theology and philosophy being set free, and the rethinking storm that ensued, — neither this nor the intention to tell what happened, should be allowed to suggest it is anything but a cul-de-sac of Development. Self does not stay with it. There is only "The Way'.

Development VI

MANY ENLIGHTENED?

One aspect of 'seeing', was that despite being awake through the medium of the human brain, homo sapiens is not central in the dharma's eternal dance, and Tennyson's "a thousand types are gone," is there to be accepted.

Even when Evolution was first understood it became concerned with the rise of man to his 'prime' position at 'the top of the developmental pyramid'.

Humanity has seen itself in a unique position, but this view has been challenged, and the loss of being so special will need to be grieved.

At the moment, thousands of species are becoming extinct annually as environments change rapidly, and many species that are successful now will evolve to something new.

Of the eternal dance, the cockroach and the human both have their own part, their own pirouettes, share the becoming, and hold everything in their nature. However, the view put forward in these pages: that the dancing, movement, change is all there is, is yet another cause for grief.

So also, is the developing crisis of our planet. Human over-population, and competition for space and environment brings strong feeling and urgency. Yet in optimal numbers humanity might lead and nurture.

However, competing with each other for food and territory and exploiting other species who share our destiny will leave homo sapiens with a wasted planet. This must be known while there is time.

It is easy to berate this opinion, as if holding it leads to intrusion without ethics and betrayal of precepts. Neither extreme is appropriate, but two elements are of proven value: respect for contraception throughout the culture, and the education of women.

So what sort of conservationist does all this produce? It is happening already? People are stepping from their central place, realising that an increasing population exploiting the biosphere is leading to despoilment of the habitat of many creatures, and soon the whole planet.

Many who respect Nature with a capital 'N' have an intuitive sense of the dharma. They are not personifying, but are intuitively aware of the dynamic aspects of everything. This intuition about the dangers to their planet is real.

There are hundreds of thousands whose 'sight' does not belong to a formalised system of religion, and this is so whether or not they would call it 'enlightenment' or realise its implications. Having credibility is their problem.

However, if this is only partly understood, it can lead to pseudo-religion, a worship of 'Nature', particularly 'Nature' unchanged by civilisation.

This latter would be a denial of man's potential for knowledge and protection of Earth and our co-inhabitants, a denial of man's development that cannot be turned back, and a denial of the common quality of motorcycle and wetland, of man's unity with his biosphere. And the worship of Nature in this limited sense ignores the implications of 'sight'.

On the planet Gniidix, many adults of one species might be Buddhas: a society beset by curiosity about how much of Self they are unaware.

Development VI

Buddhism as a Philosophy

Philosophers like to classify views of Reality and Buddhists must accept they will do so. When the insight of Just This and nothing else' comes as a result of meditation, what is This? As Hui-nêng said "The bell is ringing in your head."

This is at first view an 'idealist' philosophy, which term is misleading: it really means as 'idea-ist', derivative of 'idea', although it is 'ideal' in the 'mental process', 'spiritual sense'.

Yet 'idea-ist' philosophies do not stand up to much testing, particularly when there is confusion about whose ideas we are talking about.

It is only when the total oneness is known and 'no boundaries' is utter, that the idealist nature of Buddhist philosophy makes sense. So when the goose is 'out', the boundaries of skull and skin are down, and the consistency of it all is testable, it is a special 'idealist' philosophy.

Like Teilhard's philosophy it is also termed 'Monist'. "Total oneness' philosophies are called 'monist', but this term misleads. It implies 'material existence', and, as such, connotes 'something' and process. It allows absolute pantheism and reduces 'Emptiness/ 'no thing' to a classified concept.

Not only does 'monism' not express the wonder of Mind, and all its dynamic creatures, it ignores the potential for creation, development, and the complexity of Suchness, but if it can still be called 'monism' it is a special form of monism' that is both 'Science' and 'Sunyatta'.

While Zen Buddhism is not 'dualist' in any respect, it is certainly — naturalist, in contradistinction to 'supernaturalist' Seemingly, there is a contradiction between idealist and naturalist philosophies.

But the physicist through quantum mechanics also has a view. 'The event' is correlated processes in nerve tissue. What type of experiment is used, as well as perceptual set and interpretation, also contribute to 'the event'?

Our physicist would say that a virtual state has been registered in the nervous system. This quantum event has been complemented by the sum of quantum events having effect on the nervous system, and 'Realness' is given to it by that changing representation, but. which of the virtual states contributes is always uncertain. The seeming stability is due to the juxtaposition of millions of events in parallel.

It is a physics of wave function, and perception of wave function as motion or 'stillness' of 'particles', depending on the observing nervous system. It is thus both 'idealist' and 'naturalist', but not implying that the physics of Mind has any special order apart from organisation and complexity, when compared with any other aspect of matter / energy / spacetime studied.

And, as a whole, every wave and change inter-related, consistent even in its uncertainty.

So we could term Buddhism: **'idealist' / 'monist', 'naturalist'** and, as such, subject to testing for consistency, and **contra materialist.**

Yet the philosopher who struggled with the contradictions of this, and made meaning of these words from his own discipline, would still have to find 'the way' from the beginning. Again, his paradox will be with an idealism that is both science and Sunyatta **where there is no distinction between idealism and realism.**

This is because it is the idealism at the 'collapse' of the wave function at the photographic plate of brain process that produces the wonderful illusions: all one process optimal for the survival of life.

There is a story about a young woman who had been sitting in a determined and persistent manner for a long time. She rose suddenly with great joy. She saw clearly. What she said was, "the wall meets the floor"

She 'saw' what a philosopher might take a whole book to argue. In The Awakening of Zen, D.T. Suzuki illustrates this unity with the mutuality of a man and a flower. He only points at the singleness of Heaven and Earth.

The idealism/realism experiment occurs naturally in everyday life, or can readily be contrived.

Consider Canute's legendary experiment: the sea laps at the royal toes as he tries to keep the tide back by royal command or even royal will.

Did he take off his shoes? The water was cold. His lateral spino-thalamic tracts are working hard: countless thousands of impulses going rostrally to his brain. Brain, skin, sand, water, all doing "their thing together".

There are many variations, and those who drive well on the freeway do so because they have had a *kensho* on this issue. They might not put it that way, but their intuition is sound nontheless.

Development VI

Finding 'a way'

The modern teacher Robert Aitken uses the given of modern quantum mechanics 'complementarity', to help avoid confusion for those testing 'The Way'.

While 'The Way " is such as it is, and all opposites are One, so Emptiness and Differentiation are also One. In the traditional poetic form: "Sunyatta is The Ten Thousand Things; The Ten Thousand Things are Sunyatta"

In a modern form: 'emptiness' and the processes perceived as 'everything' are two aspects of complementarity as waves and 'particles' are in physics.

The Middle Way experienced by Nagarjuna is an expression of this complementarity. Nagarjuna's focus was on nirvana and samsara, identity and differentiation: he saw all philosophical assertions as void because all experience was relative.

> During 1987 the opportunity arose to learn more about back disabilities. There was knowledge about anatomy and mechanics of the back. There was teaching about the spine's function in many practical situations.
>
> For all the acceptance of wearing the brace from first dressing in the morning, to going to bed at night, the possibility of having a self-supporting back again had never been totally given up.
>
> Seriously performing the exercises, then transforming them into a yoga came naturally. Many weeks passed and the back became more supple and gradually much stronger.
>
> After some months the back brace with its four steel strips was left in the cupboard one Saturday morning, when there was no work for two days.
>
> There was pain, some setbacks; persistence was required. The brace was not worn again. The muscles and joints functioned much better. The exercises are a yoga and way': an opportunity for samadhi, a practice that continues.

The Clothes of 'Seeing'

'Seeing' and having simpler habits of mind changes the feelings. They are transformed to energy. They gather to energy and action and are gone.

A book leaves us with the limitations of words. As the writer puts letter after letter to paper or screen, he or she is attempting to convey all that the parallel processors of his brain can do at once in 'seeing': a multimedia of picture in motion, concepts in subsumed networks, data and feeling: to reduce it to letters: to stimulate a similar process in the reader?

No. It is impossible. Yet one of the advantages of sequential words on a page is to prod and provoke. "There is a way; you'll find it."

So, this book will 'become.'

Words will not really show anybody 'The Way', only say there is one, and the effect of it is demonstrable.

While adapting Shakyamuni's awakening to the Twentieth and Twenty-first Centuries might seem desirable, 'suchness' will develop as it develops. Just as 'seeing' was inevitable and the ironies often funny.

DEVELOPMENT VII

THE RAFT

To 'see' 'This which is Utterly One': curiosity — how does it go around?

What to do with 'sight'? For Whom?

And do it directly, forget the words in development and have heart for what must be done?

Some masters would secure the view, all sasshos to the koan — make the right view true, clear and comprehensive. Teaching needs be such as to maintain curiosity, awareness, and eventually full acquaintance with the dharma, indeed to prevent it being lost or presented in a way that the awareness would become phony, superficial or ritualised.

While that is vital and mandatory for a teacher, there is nobody to do it, no mind to plan it, and no place from which to take a view, only waves pounding on the beach, yet authentic teaching brings further 'sight' and example to lift others out of suffering.

To teach, however, would be to stay in the river of words, even though words, like 'sound', 'emptiness', 'clapping' and 'seeing' are used and attain a new meaning through intuition, they are there as a provocative approximation to being 'awake'.

Shakyamuni was acutely aware of this problem and drew the parallel of a raft used to cross a river: we might preserve it for others to use, but would not mistake it for our goal or carry it on our backs.

Helping others in the river of words, the sea of form, is appropriate, but not to stay in that mode, or indeed any mode. When a mode is appropriate it will be lived, when to be with no mode is appropriate....

Development VII

GET UP! KNOW YOUR FACE.

The Buddhism we know as Zen has undergone a passage through first Chinese and later Japanese and Korean culture.

Suzuki writes about the traditions: of Bodhidharma who refused to go to the King's court, and left to meditate facing a wall, and said, when asked who he was, that he didn't know; as well as of The Sixth Patriarch Hui-Nêng (638 - 713 AD) who wrote this verse upon the wall to become The Fifth Patriarch's successor:

> The bodhi is not like the tree,
> The mirror bright is nowhere shining;
> As there is nothing from the first,
> Where can the dust itself collect?

Indeed, he was not even a monk, but a kitchen hand originally inspired by The Diamond Sutra. He wrote the gatha in response to one by the heir-apparent which indicated the need for 'the mind' to be wiped clean of dust while in a quiet and pure state of meditation.

Hui-Nêng's verse was a revolution against quietist meditation, and was an assertion of 'no mind'.

Hui-nêng then retreated for many years, before he came out to train others. One of his basic questions was, "Show me your face before you were born."

He was one to look for value from every meditation, and asserted the unity of zazen and 'seeing wisdom' — *prajna*.

And the message of zen masters "You must look to the nature of yourself to know."

> "The kingdom is within you and without you;
> when you know yourselves you will be known."
> Jesus in 'The Gospel According to Thomas' 3.

Despite all the words here and elsewhere, such is the message, and Zen's tradition is to sit in meditation — the Zen counterpart of going 'out into the wilderness', an aspect of Christianity that has not become popular.

The Zen trainee, after sitting, will be called to the teacher, to say of his koan, what is he or she. Response is terse, encouragement is given subtly, but the teacher does not allow aspects of guruism to cling to himself or his office.

THE SHACKLED SELF

Teaching attracts two groups who require extensive work before they are free to develop an active self.

One group is focused upon the support of a guru (in the Western sense of 'guru').

You might say that a great example or an enlightened saying is surely an important aspect of teaching. On the other hand, the experience of gathering together in a group where the 'leader' does it all, is sought by many for its own sake.

There is a sense of requited mother love; guru and followers in mutually stroking circles — development work may be replaced by the passivity of childhood.

For the other group, the charismatic leader is required by many with unresolved personality issues from their childhood: those who were left with the need for individual mastery and glory.

A parent was like that, or demanded it of them; they were not assisted to grow from this early stage, or they had an overdose of glory themes at a critical stage of development. They cannot be free of it. They are not able to look at their self or to develop their self much at all.

They hurt with every failure and every bit of reality they must avoid or deny.

A few such go on to be flamboyant and omnipotent, but most do it in their dreams. They are attracted to the successful, the celebrated, the one who seems to be as they would be, wanting to see their ideal self in the mirror. The media plies them with examples. They are left exquisitely sensitive to the slights of ordinariness.

It is not such a leader they need, but a therapist or trusted friend who can reflect their pain and missing feelings and help them to the reward of an active functioning self.

The imagination is destructive when applied to building a would-be 'I' of mastery — and status. This 'I structure' shackles the self, feelings are stopped, and energy is applied to defences.

This would be 'I' is so inappropriate for daily life it must be closeted. The defences must not only maintain a mask to others, but hide the true nature of self from awareness. The process is hidden and the pain inescapable.

Development VII

This has come about from the necessities of childhood, and requires a gentle touch while he or she is relinquishing it.

The enmeshment with the charismatic leader may never be more graphic than when the more deeply alienated from self are caught up in a cult where the leader demands their limited resources to the point of enslavement.

They are specifically vulnerable. And it is their own glory seen in the leader that provides the cult stability at which outsiders wonder. Both compassion and deliverance are needed — but some may find their deliverance to ordinary life most painful, but that is where they might grow.

Of these two situations, the guru may be an Indian tradition — but the attraction of a caring teacher is certainly latent in all cultures. Such a loving adult caring for a child who needs to avoid pain is strong medicine indeed.

Similarly, a masterly adult striding among those who have given up their own glory, but are still locked into the glory theme, seems difficult for them to refuse. Their need for gratification is met vicariously through their identification with him.

Shakyamuni knew the dangers. Subhuti was telling him he was the greatest one who ever lived or words to that effect, and Shakyamuni asked him if he knew all the Buddhas that had preceded him, and those yet to come, and further, was he actually listening to his thought. Subhuti was given a clear message.

... SUCH A CREATURE

One medium where the question of the nature of man is examined from many directions, is in quality Science Fiction. The question most asked: does humanity have a nature sufficiently able to overcome greed and aggression, to enable care for the natural world, including other species?

In this context, how do the natural ethics that develop from 'seeing', fit with the elements of the human animal?

Consider human aggression, with its competitiveness, and the status seeking of the social animal, the tough fighter for survival of self, family and community. And the sexuality of this survivor of hundreds of millions of years of evolution? Homo sapiens has evolved from a small animal of low status to be the dominant and ubiquitous land animal of today. What quality of feeling accompanies this sexuality and aggression, and sets the priorities and energy of experience: — the power behind action?

In some manner, all of human process is imbued with feeling. We are born with the potential for these feelings and the behaviours that go with them. This feeling is both emotional experience and the sense of quality; we may be aware of it to a varying extent, and give both the simple and complex feelings names: 'elation' to 'agony'.

The simpler and most easily identifiable primary feelings such as anger, fear and sadness are most easily spoken about. When we don't ignore them, we tend to simplify them, and often take for granted the quality of a feeling, unless it is unusual, such as being aware of a sweet quality to sadness.

Movies pick up the unusual combinations that cannot safely be experienced in everyday life, such as the positive excitement of a fearful chase and the surge of 'justified rage'.

Because the aggressive are able to express their anger as part of dominant behaviours, anger is confused with aggression. Aggression is a behaviour; anger is a feeling.

This leaves those in a social field who have relatively little power, not only left with their anger, but ashamed of it. Then it may mostly be experienced as depression.

Anger may be a relatively simple feeling: a reaction when separation or loss is threatened; it lets the others know so they may change their behaviour, or it may remain because there is no way to express it against more powerful individuals or groups.

Development VII

It is the energy of such drives and feelings that may be transformed to Heart, or may be untamed and expressed in a destructive manner.

The child's development towards what we call 'emotional maturity' is essentially appropriate adaptation to the experience of strong feeling.

Nevertheless, each individual's early development may vary in many ways. Yet afterward, will be left all the childhood habits and defenses — accepted and denied.

Not only must the child adapt to fit his humanity with society, but the remnants of his early adaptations — the disasters, 'and the fear of more', are there to shape his or her character. Hidden rage, the denied desire, and the unacknowledged fear contribute also.

The wants, the fears, delusions and fantasies, dreams and imaginings, are all there as complex webs in motion — all of it Buddha-nature. Experiencing the simplicity of zazen, it is easy to forget the Buddha-nature of a frightening dream.

It is such a creature who must carry the enlightenment that has virtually been stumbled upon.

'A tale'

A journalist travelled on assignment to an island in the Indian Ocean to interview a master. Arriving at the main town he telephoned and introduced himself to the young woman who answered. He told her he was doing a 'millennium story' and that the master was one of the very few people who might give answers 'without his own angle'.

"My readers want to know."

"Yes", she said. "To know what?"

"It's the end of the millennium. There's a lot going to happen. There's a lot of people scared — insecure."

"Yes", she said.

'It's important. We need something we can use. Pictures too.

Hello! Hello!"

"Yes."

"Will he talk to me?"

"Yes. But call again when your ears are tuned. You will hear it all then."

Click.

On advice from the head porter, he went to the back bar at the local 'Country Club'.

"What's with the put-off?"

He made the barman understand why he was there.

The barman laughed.
"You're not the first. Try old Mary over there."

The movement of his head indicated a woman wearing a loose yellow outfit at a small table looking out over the golf course. "Better take her a drink. I make this special coffee for her."

She must have received some message from the barman: she was expecting him. She had big eyes. 'Fifties' he thought. "Could have taken more care with her make-up. Confident though".

"He told me I should bring you one of these."

She laughed warmly. "Thanks."

He offered her a cigarette. She refused with a grimace.

"I came to get a story from The Master," he said. "You know how to get into that place?"

She was observing him carefully over her drink.

"What do I have to do?" he asked

"I was there." she said. "Seventies, followed a guy. Not so stupid now."

Development VII

She drank suddenly. "... had a shock there I think — still getting over it. Didn't want it ... but I believe it, and this is the way it is."

"What have I got to say to get an interview? I mean coat and tie? What are the rules?"

"Can't you just make up a story like the rest of them do?" She was looking into him as if she'd known him well for years

He was irritated. "Bugger it", he said "I want to know. I can feel it coming. I want to tell it — sell it too."

"Your readers wouldn't know if it happened under their noses. They want a light show with four horsemen. They want a big deal Daddy with disaster for the judged — huge fireballs, deluges and earthquakes."

"No!" He was abrupt. "Not Revelation junkies. More the Gospel serious types. Quietly in the night types".

She smiled as if taking him seriously for the first time, but she was scornful.

"They want a presentable male, preferably white with no shit sticking to him: identifiably Christian who won't rock their boat by saying anything radical. Nothing new — nothing to change their priorities so they have to get off their butts — no new life."

He said defensively. "Everybody wants somebody of their own type."

This annoyed her. "What about one who says, "There is one God. Allah. Search within yourself to find Paradise and submit." They wouldn't accept that sort of answer would they?"

This time he laughed. "My boss wouldn't. And if".

"Or", she interrupted in a louder voice,

"Or the Jewish daughter who suddenly relaxes, smiles at her mother and says, "I have found The Temple at Jerusalem", and goes out and works with the Salvation Army."

"Nut case." He shook his head. "You're saying to me there's no way anybody knows."

"No!" It was sharp, staccato, loud, but not a shout. "They want the messenger, but the message is what counts — where to look and in what frame of mind — how to be and how to live. You can only do it yourself. But they try to escape to somewhere else when they find it. Anyway, they've all been told many times".

"Is this all they say out there?"

She actually giggled. Tears came to her eyes. "They'll try and show you — give you opportunity to find out — set you thinking sideways, but they won't tell you."

"Not good copy." He thought for a while. "This story is needed. And a lot of people are ready."

"Maybe", she said, "I doubt it."

A movement of her hand. He went and got her another drink.

He watched her for a while, then said, "I came. He is genuine and there are so many bullshit-artists."

She looked at him seriously and then said: "You've got this 'creep up in the night' feeling. That's good. But the light, the new direction: it mightn't happen 'one man' or 'one woman' just for your religion."

She looked at him hard. "... but break out all over. Ever think of that?"

"Wouldn't be the real thing." He felt a bleak wave of disappointment.

She put her cup down and moved to the chair beside him. She put her arm warmly about his shoulder. When he thought about it later, he was astounded at how natural it seemed.

"No — you don't see.", she said emphatically pointing at his chest with all four fingers of her other hand, "There is only One".

Development VII

The Noble Eightfold Path

Much is set out for a Buddhist: there are the precepts, and to develop in accord with them, the circular movement of Shakyamuni's Noble Eightfold Path.

Because of the complexities of cause and effect, The Path is not only circular, it is sometimes convoluted, even 'figure eights'. There are links — crossover points between them.

'I' may have compulsive motives that need to be known and stopped. Going back to 'right views' again: 'seeing' something anew, dealing with an aspect of 'I' will bring a change in intention, perhaps even a change in deeper unconscious motives.

There are also numerous starting points on The Path.

Mindfulness might be such, and may also be introduced at any point, indeed might be a good link for the centre of a figure eight. It is about choosing — not only about themes of Mind, but where the body is, where the senses are directed, the company and the context. It may only be turning the head to see a person's face, or using 'the Off switch' on the remote control.

But Mindfulness can be creative. The imagination can make dynamic images now of steps to good outcome, testing them as it goes.

The Path can be a framework for action.

For example: at a seeming impasse in life: conflict in the work place, or misunderstanding with a close relative: the view might be a suitable beginning — essentially to view the other as part of Self.

Next, leave aside all the contributions of 'I' to the problem, including motives, but not neglecting fairness, make this an opportunity to speak with kindness, hold in mind the important issues, take action to engage the other, wait to hear their views, back to your view again and do not be afraid — kind speech, modify your own perception and expression of it, and if there is opportunity — sit.

'The Path' is not a staircase with 'meditation' at the top step: it is flexible efficient process to defeat suffering wherever it might be, as well as to spread enlightenment.

To engage the world? To be friendly to a dog might be easy (even Joshu's dog), but what about blinkered humanity, each about their driven direction.

'Part of a tale'

"Hi." The woman standing behind the receptionist greeted him. She looked down at a list on the desk.

"We haven't made our final selection on the books. Some things come out well on radio, some don't, and we won't be able to see the photographs of the garden."

"I'm sorry."

She looked puzzled.

"Oh", he said. "The confusion may be my fault. I came very early as I wasn't sure I would find my way around the city."

She laughed good naturedly. "It must be the Zen book then."

He nodded.

She offered him coffee but he settled for tea.

"I'm afraid I haven't read it myself. In production, it isn't always possible."

She was frowning. "I've heard it is a bit way out — New Age."

"Old age" he said instantly, his eyes alert.

She tested him. "One reader gave it up and said something most uncomplimentary about it. 'Gobbledegook' actually. I've got to be sure it doesn't come out that way on radio."

Neither his demeanor nor his silence reassured her.

"Our connection tells us to take notice. What do you do or say that's new?"

"Nothing."

Development VII

"That's not what they say."

"Well, I see how Mind is pictures and sounds and smells from all this ...." He swept his right hand. "Holds onto it over this bit and the next. Tries it out and sees what it does. Aware, awake Now. It's being One. Some say Universal Self ... intricate, marvellous, timeless, and calling it 'Something' or 'Somebody' is misleading when it is only process, nothing really, and the hurt and sadness can be avoided. "

"So you take hundreds of pages to say that?"

"Yes. Wasteful, isn't it?"

"And you're right of course, and the only one who can see this?"

She was being professionally provocative, with a hint of humouring the egocentric or the mentally ill.

There was warm eye contact and each knew the other's viewpoint.

"No. There are many who see and know. Some see bits of it and want to hold onto it, or get it together better. Many who see, just get on with their lives doing their work and caring for those around them. Some will shake their heads at what's been missed. But if lost, there's a possible road to take."

'Fragment of a tale'

The switch to open-line radio was unexpected. The questioners and the host seemed to have much to say, sometimes informative and mostly interesting....

Then "Mrs Pickersgill from West Epping".

"My question ... is ... ", she said slowly, then rapidly, "What about prayer? Your sort don't say anything about prayer. Are you against it?"

"Not if it's brief and from the very heart of self. Generally, it needs much more time to get 'I' out of the way, the words to evaporate, to see what happens. You make space to allow 'The always so' to be surely here. Not a lot of words and much quiet."

Salvation

A master polished a stone. "Why do you polish the stone?", asks a monk known for his feats of long sitting. "To 'make' a mirror", replies the master.

The experience of being 'awake' in zazen is not achieved by endurance, but by awareness of the nature of 'the seeing self'.

Shakyamuni had such respect for meditation that he saw it as a powerful process, the use of which could be dangerous.

He advised entering meditation in a frame of loving kindness, and promoted its value for compassion, insight and freedom from distress and desire. He had reservations about those who could achieve feats of great concentration, achieve power and perform miracles.

Zen is simplicity; it is being grounded in body, earth and air. There are in zen aspects of living step after step: the value of work, of harmony within the family and the *sangha*, that are value in themselves: developing through 'a Way', whether the morning exercise, tending the vegetables, cooking the meal, cleaning the kitchen, in the manner one does in meditation.

One of the great values of zazen is to begin this simplicity, and then to generalise from zazen to make living itself part of 'the Way'.

The question is: Is this becoming/development to be valued in itself without total enlightenment. Is Zen a Chinese Civil Service examination of the Ming dynasty? If one doesn't 'pass', then is it all wasted?

If enlightenment is to Buddhism in this manner, then its very fabric is vitiated. It would be another frustrated desire of 'I'.

Buddhists achieve aspects of enlightenment in their own style. Whatever 'sight' develops, it is living 'the Way', following the Noble Eightfold Path, respect where respect is due, loving compassion to others, avoiding the pain brought about by desire: this is salvation.

All may be involved in Bodhisattva action. The community do not sit around waiting for 'a special one' to come and do it for them: it is done Now, and through being done Now, Development occurs: this is a central theme in the writings of Joko Beck.

'Seeing' is a bonus to this. In particular, 'seeing' Heaven and Earth are one and the same — more, finding one's timeless Self outside 'the wheel of life', and seeing the Salvation of others which they cannot yet see themselves, is blessedness itself.

Development VII

There has long been the tradition that 'seeing' must be very true for Heaven and Earth to be known as the same. Hui-Nêng would say, "If Heaven and Earth are an inch apart they are separated forever." If this is seen truly with wonder, then Heaven is familiar.

The Christian mystic of the Fourteenth Century, Mother Julian of Norwich knew this even in the maelstrom of The Black Death when a large proportion of the population were dying.

From his early enlightenment Shakyamuni indicated that all were saved from the beginning. "All beings are the Tathagata", he said. ('Tathagata' means the 'Thus Come' and implies 'the enlightened one as Absolute Self')

Salvation is also knowing that 'karma' in both traditional and New Age sense is as a bad dream from an illusory position, where time and The Ten Thousand Things are experienced as they are not.

Karma in this sense is a source of anxiety or a projection of wishes, not even to be seen as an adaptive illusion.

Let us simply keep the word to mean the action of The Utterly One as in 'Suchness', and if projected to the future, let us use it in the meaning of 'outcome'.

In Robert Aitken's book 'Encouraging Words' there is a brief bright essay on 'karma' which starts at the bottom of page 121. He speaks positively; the essay is complete in itself, so it is necessary for those interested to read it themselves.

Pain

For some there is especial pain.

When very young, but after separation has become conceivable, the fear of separation is like the fear of a helpless and violent death. For primates this innate program is protective and thus adaptive. It is the separate child's body that is ultimately protected.

Later, as his cultural learning and genetic capacity are integrated to adapt and grow to adulthood, 'I' beliefs and sense of preservation are strong. So also, is his unease and distress at his own mortality which comes as a recurring crisis.

The death of others may be experienced with distress and isolation, or as a shared experience of dignity and meaning. Many only experience death through the media. Through their defences many people still see personal death as isolating, frightening and unacceptable.

Western culture's emphasis is focused on the supremacy of the objective world and separation from it behind the skin. The protection of awareness is not available.

There is no sense of Now's validity over Then. The Deity as a Somebody seems similarly is separate and then The Body of Christ is not 'seen'. There is little questioning of the 'nature of self'.

As the self quietens its striving, sits, relaxes and accepts 'the Way', there is an opening to the Unity of what has been there all the time. There is only Self.

Eternity Now can be accepted whole, or some at a time. It is only necessary to remain open to this possibility, and be aware that the details from society already accepted may be blocking awareness of Unity.

The Not Separate is thus found.

Development VII

THE USES OF ENLIGHTENMENT

The conviction that many others will 'see' is a vital matter. And of this 'sight'? Evidence that many are enlightened in their own way is everywhere.

The commonality is recognised intuitively, the awareness of Nature, both animate and inanimate, the wholeness, power of its effects, its ways; the awareness of its change and development.

Enlightenment is in those who are aware of doing, loving and feeling as the true reality.

Enlightenment is apparent in the awareness of the oneness of man and land. This may be a house, a garden, a family farm, a beloved area of wilderness, a forest, a rock, or the whole planet. The awareness may extend to the creatures and plants that share it.

There is identification with many a creature who is so much part of its own habitat — obvious wholeness. Totem is an example of this communion with other species, and animals and birds may be symbols for armies and football teams.

As a skink in the sunshine is not oppressed by the illusion of time, eternity is known to the enlightened.

There is enlightenment in many statements about 'The World' or 'Life': such as allowing "The world doesn't owe me anything." It is 'The always so' that is being talked about.

Often 'Life' is capitalised: as in "Life has been kind to me", or "Life does that sometimes." There is enlightenment in everyday intuition that is only half realised, but unnamed.

Symbols are used because man sometimes loses sight of the communion with place, tree and creature. Symbols may distract from such sight. However, many returning home after a long absence have a direct sense of spiritual reunion.

While the enlightenment of the Zen Masters was required and traditional, the enlightenment of those with no Buddhist antecedents is a subject of great fascination.

That such enlightenment could occur was at times remarkable. Muhammed Jalal al-Din Rumi (1207-1273), referred to in these pages, came from a Sufi background within Islam during the golden years of learning, but Rumi was of an enlightened tradition of Sufis, including Prince Ibrahim b Adham (d 777 AD) who at an inner prompting left his way of life to search for self and make his living from gardening.

In the Nineteenth Century was brilliant American poet Walt Wittman with his 'Song of Myself'. It has been viewed by some as a product of psychosis, but it will set you on a rich joyful experience and a confirmation of active energetic development.

In Essays in Zen Buddhism First Series Suzuki quotes Meister Eckhart frequently as if he was one of the great Zen Masters of Tang China. Suzuki in a later book fully confirms the quality of the Meister's enlightenment. One can only imagine the effects of his 'sight' on The Fourteenth Century Church, particularly when it occurred in The Dominican Order at Cologne.

Teilhard's God of Matter is an expression of 'The always so', and Teilhard's need to personify this is seen in the Christic aspect of everything; it too is an expression of Utter Oneness. Many branches of Buddhism personify 'The always so' in a similar manner.

Similar too is Kung's view of oneness, although he would like the superior indescribable Being existing qualitatively beyond everything.

But the paramount nature of process/change, as a scientist or Buddhist would see it, is difficult to discern in his thought. Without sharing his intuitive sense, we are left requiring 'faith' and subject to agnosticism.

THE ETHICS OF ONENESS

There are natural ethics in the actions of 'Not I'.

The protection of the creek from pollution, the smile given to a child, compassion for those in jail, the saving of the small creature's habitat, all care for aspects of the total self, all development; the ethic is knowing what has to be done, and it happening.

As Mind moves, it follows naturally that how Mind moves contributes to the outcome of peace, harmony and valued experience.

So, simply, such ethic brings valuable consequences, not only for the individual and the community, but even the species or the whole biosphere.

However, if 'I' is wanting what brings inevitable suffering, because it is impossible or because it represents the narrow foolish interests of the individual without awareness, then suffering will spread.

Seeing clearly how suffering is a result of desire, provides the short cut to avoid it. Again the ethic is to promote good results.

A good example of such a Buddhist ethic is 'The Four Way Test' of Rotary International that embodies consequences of truth, fairness, benefit, goodwill and better friendships.

Such ethics are the wisdom of a culture and may be spelt out like this or intuitably shared.

Because the intrinsic nature of 'The always so' is movement, then action is the ethic rather than passivity or words.

Work — doing what is needed, shared care of others, provides a natural value above any form of parasitism. Indifference and torpor are not doing. Theorising and not helping, writing and not publishing, good intention and promises without action ....

Because knowing the nature of self leads naturally to ethics for the development of all, then this knowledge and awareness of self is immensely valuable. Its value is so great, it is difficult to conceive.

And from Self comes the recognition of quality in others, their intent and capacity. It allows of co-operative partnerships and the sharing of ideas and goodwill to bring about beneficial action.

Because 'The always so' does 'its thing' through partnerships and families, teams and congregations, the shared thought and deeds have a puissance for good outcome beyond the capacity of one body.

Because well directed zazen achieves right perception, biological energies are diverted. Inherent drive and feelings are now the energy of development.

This is the 'Heart' that energises the apprentice to express the Buddha. This is the hope that harmony and 'Oneness of being' is the direction of development.

When enlightened perception can see the essential from the non-essential then desire or evil action may be circumvented.

Because 'seeing' allows choice, cause and effect are shattered.

As 'seeing' becomes whole, the guilt of cause and effect evaporates, but what is there instead is the widest of choices as to how karma will flow. All the virtual directions, shadings of action, may become real in the illumination of 'the seeing self'.

This brings the broadest responsibility. It is where cause and effect stops, and in its place is Ethic — the channel through which good outcome springs from virtual directions to the future. 'I' the illusion, is sacrificed as ignored. 'Not I' sees and becomes.

Then the circular process of The Noble Eightfold Path is readily followed to spreading circles of good outcome. Right Livelihood and Right Action are 'catching'.

This is the inexorable movement of Unitary Ethics (Natural Ethics of The Utterly One) and it enables avoiding bad karma as it sweeps in the circles of effect to effect.

> The young widow has taken her children on a pilgrimage around the world. In Nepal, she stays in an Ashram to meditate. She is finding herself and peace. One day she finds her belongings are all stolen. She goes to the teacher. "Must I accept even that?", she asks.
>
> "That is not the teaching." He is decisive. "You do not accept that which is bad karma for you and the thieves." With right action her belongings were returned, and she and her family continued their journey.

Development VII

It is like the lotus flower — as each petal from the inside to the edge is well formed, so is the flower.

Bad karma may come about from thoughtless or foolish action. Further than bad karma is the active process of evil. 'Evil' is a problem word and a distressing concept to secular Late Twentieth Century society, and is generally only spoken in judgemental tones by people not respected by the man or woman in the street.

There is denial about it, just as there has been about other emotive issues such as 'sex' and 'death'. As there is not an alternative word however, its use needs be continued.

In this context evil is a differentiated process of destructive action, cyclically bringing further destruction, and passing through individual and society alike. It is not chaos. The patterns of chaos are well represented in 'The always so'; they have their own beauty.

Rather, evil is suffering born of isolation, detachment and malign desire, generating further suffering. The mix of fear, hurt, and a desire for vengeance, generates evil whether in the helpless or the powerful.

Evil is different from 'the opposites' in that it actively makes its own destiny. It has the contradistinction — 'not evil'. Simple thought would see 'good' opposed to evil. However, evil is difficult to oppose, 'good' is relative and may even provoke it. 'Not evil' needs to be flexible and active: perceive the circumstance, appropriate action may be open engagement or subtle: whether containment, care, damage control, alternatives, brave example, or kindness for hostility.

But evil is superfluous to 'The Way'.

"Original Love"

Man required aggression, and a spectrum of strong drives and emotional responses to compete in every sea and jungle of our evolution. When these adaptive drives are subverted to individual aggression, this gives the illusion of 'original sin'.

In balance to this, or even despite it, is the human species — capable of succour, love, ethics and modern democracy.

These qualities come through even in a situation of overpopulation and depleted resources, because humanity has evolved as a social species with order and organisation, protecting the — community and its land.

Sometimes the individual seeking status, striving single-mindedly to climb the ladder of his group, is a greater innate problem than overt aggression. It may produce more 'I consciousness' than individual survival. Yet this status struggle brings order and evolution, ultimately bringing structure to the village and the nation.

This is an aspect of group function. Unfortunately, when this is unchecked, humanity is vulnerable to rigid social systems including totalitarianism.

The evolution of the larger brain to form elaborate four-dimensional maps to construe the past and anticipate the possible future, is mankind's 'Tree of Knowledge". Many choices, as well as regret, guilt, hope, elaborate expectations are all now an aspect of man's functioning.

Man's 'fall' is rather a big increase in moral vulnerability that has come with his evolution.

On the other hand, together with 'original sin', man has positive aspects from his evolution as a social animal and by being nurtured as a functioning culture prescribes.

The positive social attributes are destroyed when the young child is highly insecure, subject to sadism, and has examples of hostility, exploitation and indifference. As Erik Erikson has indicated, such a disaster can befall a nation.

The dynamic movement of the whole society is paramount. If the adaptation of a culture to a hard or depleted environment includes harsh treatment of its children, prescriptions for child-rearing that deny the child's very nature, or leave the child in a helpless situation, then evil is introduced.

This may readily occur with rigid societies, or where dogma is defended vigorously despite the suffering of the people.

Development VII

The Buddhist notion of the child being essentially good, developing with his destiny as part of the changing of the everything, and throughout life gaining special merit for initiative, sat easily with understanding of the nature of man and woman.

It compared well with the professional position: secure the child's early development: goodness will happen. However, many cultures exhort 'the not good' to be 'good', or try to change them when their beliefs and habits are established. This is mostly not useful.

But there are those without okay experience, credible example or hope, who can still find all three of these qualities.

In those who do not find them, are often seen distortions of the rage, the aggression and exploitation that have been required as part of our evolutionary development; these may be applied in concert with greed and envy from a 'not good enough' childhood.

If the child is deprived, starved of social interaction, and his or her adult not adequate, then greed and envy replace closeness and gratitude.

Greed and envy are fundamental aspects of what is known as evil. They arise in a great cycle of deprivation, failure of nurture, poor example and unformed intimacy.

They are linked to a culture's child-rearing beliefs and practices; they are nourished by ignorance and compounded by lack of resources and overpopulation. This is the trigger to man's vulnerability.

Becoming

Many become enlightened, become aware of their identity, allow 'science method' to be a process to find consistency of 'Just this', share with their fellows, and together are kind action itself: the population of the human species is at an equilibrium with the requirements of other species and resources, and enlightenment becomes everyday, equivalent to growing up: one morning a young woman says "This is truly a pure land."

This is only a tale. The reason is, that although dreams and imaginings have their own Buddha-nature, for shared karma they must leave their virtual state through action, effort and livelihood.

Development VII

Enough II

'Enough' is a pivotal theme. In the milieu of 'enough', greed and envy are irrelevant. Support for fellow humans and the other creatures who share this small planet, depends on the plague of humans being halted.

It depends on an equilibrium between the number of humans being born and those dying, which does not rely on warfare, starvation, infanticide, or a killer micro-organism.

An extension of our ethical principles to this problem is required. An ongoing alternative is needed, or we are faced with a polluting plague where homosapiens outgrows the capacity of the environment, its numbers approach a critical state, disaster provoking disaster in an unpredictable chain reaction.

Moral strength requires the addressing of this issue. Leadership is required. A Buddhist might point to 'The Middle Way' as an ethical theme of life.

A Buddhist is committed to truth from a kilo of rice to enlightenment. Yet he would be able to find a middle way when gratuitous truth would be frank cruelty and lead to bad consequences. The middle way is his natural alternative to greed, and the notion of 'enough' is basic.

Extremes are rarely appropriate, and even though this first developed in considering 'asceticism' versus 'licentiousness', it is a general mode to deal with the relative and the complex.

IMPLICATIONS

Buddhism does not reject good and bad, but espouses the acceptance of them existing together, both being aspects of quality: 'good quality' from one point of view, not so from another.

It is the direction of process that is salient; not only the quality experienced by an individual, but also the quality shared and agreed upon by significant groups and the quality of their informed hope.

The development of Unitary Ethics is enabled by seeing the true nature of 'good and bad', 'gain and loss', 'deep and shallow', and all other parameters apparently divided to poles and opposites: — they are all aspects of The One.

'Seeing' beyond verbal variables enables the virtual outcomes to be considered without arbitrary or rigid confinement. Such ethics are able to deal with more complex problems such as the quality of life for an ill person in the family, or the security of a young child, or how to relate to a man who has just been mugged. They are principled — but, dynamic principles.

As complex events unfold, dynamic principles allow actions bringing good, mixed, and neutral quality outcomes, always being aware that the true outcome is shaped by the ethical quality of the actions taken along the way.

Buddhism, however, does not have them parcelled up separately with a gulf between them, does not divide absolutely. "It's an ill wind that blows nobody any good", is understood.

It is more a commitment to value being judged in a total manner, and it will vary with the point of view, and the mixture of 'good outcome' and 'not good outcome' perceived to be present.

The attention to personal behaviour is focused on learning from experience to better value the action that makes good consequences in the broad sense. This is acceptance of The Way — the attributes of The Dharma — 'The always so'. If a child is being abused by an adult who himself or herself was abused, it is everybody's business to care for both of them.

While some ethics come naturally from the nature of 'The always so', others are implications of Self being 'awake'.

The biological nature of Man has complex elements for nurture and support for other members of the family, community and nation. On the other hand, social behaviour has elements of competition, aggression, and dominance/submission.

Development VII

They are directed at land, food supplies, shelter, mate security and status. These may be fought over, by one or two, a family, a group or a nation.

These elements of animal behaviour have been necessary for the species to evolve and survive. Nevertheless, the ethics of Oneness: 'doing', 'heart': require the flowing of these evolved energies to good outcome for all.

And when they are so transformed, what unbridled energy, and what freedom from inertia and depression?

The similarities between Christian and Buddhist ethics are seemingly remarkable.

The Buddha was clear about non-violence and love for the neighbour, and Shakyamuni's own return to his father's house is a version of 'The Prodigal Son'.

The common sense, 'Do unto others as they would wish', from a 'seeing' point of view becomes "Do unto others as you would have them do unto you."; however, without 'sight', this has led to forced conversion and 'saving souls' by violence.

'Thy neighbour as thyself' is an inevitable implication of Oneness. Notice the action word 'do' being primal in pivotal Christian ethics.

The Ten Grave Precepts, as Buddhism's 'Commandments', encourage positive dealings with others: loving, truthful, forgiving, generous, communication to be gentle and significant, and sex not to be misused.

Killing, theft and rape are not accepted, nor is altering Mind with drugs, and, as well, there is a focus on avoiding destructive attitudes such as envy and malice, and their communication by destructive gossip, lying, abuse and slander. They are similar to those delivered to Moses, but, with a New Testament seasoning.

Entering 'The Kingdom of Heaven' is similar to the attaining of nirvana. Had Shakyamuni said, "I am the way, the truth and the life", the response would have been "Of course."

These similarities might obscure the differences:

A Buddhist is of One
is aware of the unity/continuity of life
is ethical
because he/she is Self utterly
accepts Self as natural
does not want or expect the dualism of supernatural process
is aware of the salvation of The Four Noble Truths
practices the Noble Eightfold Path
rejects ignorance
experiences the truth of meditation and embodies it from waking to sleep
relates Now to these people here — all of them:

Self does not abide with form and other discrimination
finds a middle way to good consequences
thinks no evil
and is positive in seeking good outcome
but would recognise evil because of his perception
transforms the emotion of experience to creative and compassionate Heart

With the ethics there are more similarities.
We could chant:

In dealings with all, let us find a middle way and avoid extremes.

Let us hope without desire, and may the intuitive sense of quality Now not desert us.

May we only bring loved children into being and honour their growth. May protection of the powerless and the young be without reservation.

May we protect the well-being of our mate in all respects.

May we share this world with other creatures and their homes, acknowledging their entitlement to make their living without destruction as we are entitled to make our living.

May we keep air, soil and water clean for all.

May those who seek a loving parent in the dharma find Him or Her.

May the awareness that all are neighbours be held surely.
May we provide and accept forgiveness freely.

Let us respect the useful illusions but not be fooled by their nature.

Let the self be well adapted to the requirements of this life.

May the character of this life contain the distresses of Reality.

May we be aware enough of the feelings of others that our speech and actions are experienced by them as kind.

May we accept and value the processes of The Always So and know the futility of wanting more.

When we test the nature of the dharma may we avoid the bias of our wishes.

Let us act in a manner to bring good karma in extending waves.

Let us accept the manner of religious development of others and keep from unwanted preaching at their door.

May we share the peace and power of emptiness.

WHAT COMES 'NEXT'?

Many Buddhist traditions are focused on reincarnation. Indeed the preoccupation with karma and rebirth from the old religions of the Indian subcontinent is seen by many as 'Buddhism'. With the Buddha's enlightenment this was bypassed.

There are now popular teachings about guided rebirth, and of continuity of consciousness from one life to the next. Some are 'New Age' and others from respected lines of Buddhism.

While The Utterly One is conscious and conscious and conscious, and all beings are Self: so the answer to the rebirth question is "Of course!": there are many problems in the old beliefs.

These are about wanting permanence for an aspect of consciousness, of not being aware of the 'idealist' nature of 'realism', *and how the process Mind is grounded in the others called blood, brain and breath.* To give consciousness a different status to other processes is a return to body / mind dualism. This makes a distinction between such 'surviving processes', and processes that are buns and trees and emit noises like "Wu".

Zen is indeed fortunate that Wen-yên had his leg caught in the gate.

And it is inevitable that even a religion which promotes enlightenment will have the problem of its traditions and structures exposed to 'sight'.

'Seeing' is seeing past the shape of things and other notions. As they are all of The One, the attitude comes from source: day to day wisdom: this food is edible, the wind is cold, and that data requires a new hypothesis: but the unity prevails.

This also applies to what comes first, second and third. Shakyamuni 'saw' that the origin of every process was dependent on those that came before.

When the waves of cause and effect, whatever their origins, come to break upon 'seeing', all the virtual wavelets of the bay might develop. But 'Sight' allows new thoughts, new action, with complex and uncertain effects.

With the sense of unity and an ethical attitude, 'seeing' allows immense flexibility of action. Any of the virtual actions that might occur can be done. Cause and effect might be hijacked, or turned back on itself, or its cycles changed.

Shakyamuni took hold of The Wheel. His 'sight' and compassion have come to us over twenty-five centuries.

Development VII

Many cannot bear not knowing the future. There is a swell of demand to know the outcome linked to a variety of fears and wants.

But predictions are for the actuary. The 'butterfly's wing effect' arouses new interest. Mind in its communicative suchness: the possibilities — thousands to the six-billionth power — "Well. Approximately: there are that many people?": prophecy is that great a wank.

Yet Utter Oneness is as valid in time as in space.

A nine-year-old patient said, "When I want to go somewhere, I'd like my body to just appear at the other place." She said this because she intuitively knew 'no boundary' in the time dimension, and was wishing it was not so.

While everybody knows that a safe journey is necessary for continuance at the destination, or that they have arrived safely on the journey from conception, it seems difficult for them to see the implications of this experiment. So Utter Oneness is not obvious.

When asked about this by a Buddhist friend, the pen scratched two drawings: one of a large aeroplane on the tarmac, but its silhouette divided by a control tower in the foreground, the other of the questioner at one point in time and another later, with a large space in between. He sees much, lives wisely, and brings the health of his *sangha*.

'A tale'

The friend has sat bravely. Emptiness is true and full of energy. He is learning not to be afraid of his 'sight'.

This time he approaches from the other direction: He asks: "I see the mind perceiving all it makes of 'waveforms and nerve impulses' — that nothing. But the waveforms of photons: the standing waves — electrons and the uncertain processes of atomic nuclei: that energy — which is mostly consistent when you test it, but only virtual until you do.

Is it a different nothing?

Then he laughed.

'... AND THE POLITICS'

When a dictator or elite, overpower or brainwash the individual in the name of society, and leave the aspirations of the people and the family aside, use control, power and arms in the name of the nation, and glorify collective strength, then entrapment, cruelty and oppression grow.

When individuality is glorified, and the young and weak are not given protection from exploitation, assault and debauchment by strong individuals driven by greed and the will for power and gratification, then entrapment, cruelty and oppression grow.

Such factors may be mixed in confused anarchy or be somewhere along the continuum between these two.

The Rule of Law and mutual assistance will develop internationally, but slowly.

'Another tale'

The man had come West after his relationship had broken up. He was unhappy and depressed. In his first weeks at the zendo he seemed refreshed by his sitting and much calmer.

Then his blacker mood returned. He burst out to the group: "The birds in fuckin' Montana. Cats and coyotes! And everybody South! All of it! Unreal!", he shouted. "What good is it?"

The master moved quietly to his side. "It is the way it is." There was some emphasis on 'way'.

His voice rose: "But not groups and platoons; towns and cities: it's people hurting: people matter!"

The master put her right hand on the front of his shoulder and turned him towards her.

"This morning', she said. "What happened to the spider?"

"You picked it up ... took it outside ... put it on the tree." "Yes", she said.

Development VII

"Maria was scared of it."

The master widened her eyes to him and he knew.

More to the others she said, "Even the smallest things come in quanta. Each its own little bundle."

"Is it done with ... ?"

Are there special places where feelings of great mystery and wonder make one experience awe? And give a special quality to meditation?

A garbage tip under a night sky? Rotui capped with cloud? Tranquillity Base? Thirty-seven Popov St on a Thursday afternoon in January? Or the mat in the back room?

Is it done with icons? Crystals? Cobblestones? Or relics? Bullshit is a saleable commodity.?

And word forms: the nembutsu, the mantra, The Apostles' Creed: are soundless sounds that are necessary?

They will be.

A Buddhist temple may bring families together and underline their blessing, but inherent is the appreciation of Oneness, the body in which it was first symbolised, the pathfinder, the lighthouse. But this finds/is The Buddha.

DEVELOPMENT VIII

The Shadows

'seeing'

can miss the foreground

may not gain attention

the habits of the social niche

occupied

for so long

involved

with what does not matter

preoccupied

held with the same apparent

FORMS

the changes of no mind
there is neither form
nor formlessness
It is

the apparent form of illusion
that does not matter
more

the form of illusion might confused
distract from what is important
words and other symbols
might be confused with
seeing directly

a form might be desired
time wasted chasing the shadow

the essence missed

Development VIII

REST AND COMFORT

the immensity of doing
loving   giving   developing

ignored

while drowning in an ocean of dualist words

a deep ocean

'this and that'   'you and I'   'here and there'

'now' and 'then'

'I'

is an example of form elaborated

'I' is built of convictions
about the characteristics and status of 'I'
and representative objects
the illusion 'I'
generates more illusion 'I'

a society
builds group and national myths
to give such 'I' factors form

form is sought
form is a distraction
that leads away from doing
form is the illusion to hide change

form is a collection of would-be anchors

or a collection of anything else
form is 'that' and 'that'

form dominates thought
worries have elaborate form
form overruns social action
and 'form' chasing more form
is devoted to aggression and magic

form in behaviour

can be an alternative to natural ethics

cruelty is marked by form

form is often the object of desire

        and as such
is closely linked
    with transience and suffering

form is as dangerous when imagined
      as when it is concrete
wishful thinking and a desire for magic solutions
are particularly precarious attempts
      to adapt

they seem to carry people
above the rapids of life

yet increase their pain
as there is further to fall

sometimes the rise of wish and magic
represents a socially acceptable form of greed

as a young woman said
    at a crisis in her psychotherapy
      "Reality is not enough"

Form does not only refer to triumphal arches

it refers to the form of manners

and the form of teaching and religious expression

form may be bound in the shape of books
      and within them
    is the binding of language

Development VIII

      when there is an attempted understanding of the dharma
            some struggle with 'Nothing'
    they see form where there is only process
               impose form on emptiness
      they are not the action of
           The Ten Thousand Things
              which is truly empty
                    are not 'Change' aware of Itself

whether form is a word or a mandala
abiding with
         form
             does
                 not
                     create

        as a conjurer's fingers create illusion

    form distracts from emptiness

so the peace and truth of emptiness are not available

        and rest and comfort are lost

LE WEEKEND

some experiment with language
others abide with the form prescribed
by their teachers or tradition
there is preoccupation with *le weekend*
becoming part of the French language
and more interest in spelling

sequential verbal language is glorified
above other forms of expression
it is as if the form of expression has a validity
above that which is expressed
it may be deemed   logic   rhetoric

it is not coincidence that magic power
is said to abide in a word
or 'spell' the common English word for an incantation
or its supposed effects   in fantasy   words are power
prophecy spells out the changes of power-
the frightened are gullible
when the ignorant talk of changes yet to come
self-fulfillment is inevitable
prophecy is a bridge from suffering to more suffering

the shaman and the charlatan prey upon the foolish
better The Great Mumford and "peanut-butter sandwiches"

communication of insight
of gestalt appreciations
is not suited to words
the word 'love' is a wraith of 'loving'
but to persevere in a written mode is important
when it is the only alternative
but the words are only a tool   and their form
a reflection in a pond
find the real thing

Development VIII

and 'the word' can become enshrined

the Tripitaka and the Bible
when treated as icons
rather than as communication of aspects of spiritual truth
can not only distract
but become forms to be addressed in their own right
as if the words are not just symbols
pointing to the way
the words are worshipped
not to change with the language of the people

a sect can schism
over a change in emphasis on aspects of a scripture
different articles of faith
a gulf can be created with alternative meanings

a scientist may know
what happens at the boundaries of a black hole
but the words to describe it
might not be able to convey his insight
on the other hand
a student experienced in theoretical physics
who looks at the jottings
can experience that knowing

Roles or the Real Thing?

mysticism is a form
to Western societies 'a mystic' is a role
journalese to describe
somebody highly atypical of the group
but with original preoccupations
which are not understood
yet notable for that reason
and if there is awareness
of the nature of 'The always so'
the unitary nature of the dance
he or she is so tagged

it easily becomes esoteric
supernatural
  a 'big-deal'
     and develops the isolation of elitism
         on the other-hand if it is not beyond science
            then it is not interesting
                journalism requires it to be grand and inexplicable

The Scientific American in the early seventies
ran an exhaustive article
on glory phenomena observed in mists
this is not the stuff of a popular story
yet a secular mind without much training
can have a reasonable notion
of the interaction of mist droplets
and light so experienced

yesterday's miracle
becomes today's science

there are many following the teaching
and example of others
to a knowing of 'The always so'
what they find
the effect of their new identity
on their attitude
and the natural ethics that come into being
might be extraordinary
but if it is likely to be focused upon
given a form that is unreal then
it is to be repulsive
mockery of everyday pragmatic vitality

Development VIII

"No bells ring ... "

religiosity is a social expression of a species relating to the meaning of everything

        it is a solace and comfort
        it is necessary and unnecessary
        it may be shared
        have dignity and ritual
        provide awe or inspiration

it does not change The Way one bit
and because it is necessary it continues

more will understand 'The always so'
they will be simple
they might be quite ordinary
no bells ring when they walk along the street
they will have no title
except perhaps
to distinguish their role as teacher

will they live in a monastery?   will they have a priestly life style?
one test for them will be to take their understanding to work
        to the street   to their family
will they shout about it?   proselytise?
how does their 'seeing' stand up to being in a crowd?
does it evaporate before social interactions?
can it be intimate?
does it push twosomes apart?   or can it survive closeness?
        eat baked beans on toast?

herein lies the new struggle   to be there for others
who strive to develop   but not to be a curiosity?
        not a focus of dependence
        not News

here is the value of being a peacemaker
to smile
        to speak kindly
                to be true at heart

"What is the Buddha?"
a master answered "The one in the hall."

Development VIII

SHE KNOWS THERE IS NOTHING ELSE.

zen has become the quick path   existence after existence
        to be nearer to enlightenment
        is stepped through in a stride

zen followed to all its implications strips and strips the veneers of religiosity
from the religion that pivoted from a man sitting beneath a pipal tree

to have a religion   is a tree necessary?   a fig tree particularly?
symbol or shade   communication or throne?   a figure centre stage?
the male lead?   form once more   firewood or doorstop?

a Buddha does not sit under a tree
she spreads her leaves to her light
      she flowers
           she is scented music and moonlight

when she is called a Buddha for the want of a better label
    it misleads
          there is no such thing as a Buddha

    she is not a Buddha because of her sitting   she is awake

she is not a Buddha
      because she has practiced zazen for many years
            she is zazen itself

she is not a Buddha because she is silent
            she is silent to avoid confusion

not a Buddha because of effort   at an obstacle   she is energy
        she laughs at negation

she is not a Buddha
      because she has drawn now and timelessness together
         she knows there is nothing else

when she hears talk of a Buddha, she goes on with her work

she does not seek emptiness   it is her peace and her power

her energy/compassion is like a thunderstorm

her smile engulfs the orbit of Mars

the reader cannot find her   only experience her

Development VIII

... TO LOOK THROUGH THE LUGGAGE

to teach zen would be very difficult

consider the teachers of autistic children
        they patiently work with children
        who have no readily discernible potential for learning
        but the teachers gradually find behaviours to reward
        they have some inkling of different process
        at least as it is portrayed outwardly
        and by reinforcement they channel behaviour
        where learning might be
                the by-product of the activities pursued   succeeding
                      feeling good at each step

but those who are bright and successful
they want understanding and peace
yet they must unlearn and undo
habits and conditioning
status and competition
even the thinking about personal identity
so hard won in earlier development
and most of all
understanding and peace

what they need is 'Bay 13' at the Melbourne Cricket Ground
there are a select group of barrackers
(vocal supporters, sport enthusiasts
who usually play cricket and football themselves
despite what the journalists say about them)
who gather
at a particular part of the old concrete stand called Bay 13
(at the time of revising it has been pulled down   yet survived)
they are a litmus paper for 'I-ness'
'I-ness' offends them
are acutely sensitive to its manifestations
for reasons many and obscure
they will even see 'I-ness'
where it is not apparent to others or perhaps non-existent
which is a cause of pain to capable sportsmen
from other countries
surely those upon 'The Way' need help from such a group

Development VIII

Australians sometimes call themselves 'knockers'
or 'choppers of tall poppies'
and journalists plead for that mentality to stop
but 'chopping' sells newspapers

yet the sceptics will not become gullible
the litmus response to 'I-ness' is triggered
and from their own sensibilities
whatever the reasons   such 'I-ness' is unacceptable

they are needed to look through the luggage

Development VIII

... IS

... is ordinary
day to day
'this' then 'this'
forged in the fires of ridicule
satire   irony
a 'put-down' in caustic comedy
needs Andrew Denton or John Cleese
rather than Billy Graham
naive as Big-bird
hot doughnuts and laughter
ordinary its stuff
plain pedestrian now
and step by step acceptance of 'The suchness of The Always So'

Doing

if one thinks his hand can be taken
and words used to explain it to him he will not develop
if he thinks it is impossible to develop then he will not
the general direction can be pointed
for those who are aware of the pointing hand
and then
would change their posture accordingly

apprentices at play with words   and a multitude departs
                        the confusion caused
might make them lose sight
of the only direction
in which they can go to be true
this is within what is usually called their self
for want of a better name
it is this nervous system
that must finally bring together what is needed

to say how long you sat?   to say with what view?   what to see?
sitting is a limited resource   while you sit
a blind woman grinds millet
two orphans walk on a muddy road   automatic weapon fire
and a starving child eats rice
to see' is to do   doing   no thing
and suchness is as suchness does   no mind
      doing

DEVELOPMENT IX

... ALL THERE IS ANYWAY

(i)

Together
When concentration is entirely upon the other
taking in his or her communications 'now'
diminishing
preconception or projection
practice is relaxed
unstudied
close and clear

It is natural and gratifying
to live and work with others
but when learning
difficult   to be Self in a small crowd
It is our lot   nonetheless
Do it naturally   don't try to test hypotheses
leave the theories
and what might happen next
as well as   the reflected notions about
individuals

        just be zazen
        all there is
        anyway
        let it happen

Development IX

                        (ii)

Walking through the shopping mall?
The posture and the breathing in the walk
            With nowness
     coping with all sensations

like many stereos turned on at once — and
then
     the oneness
          energy
               peace
                    loving
                         wonder

                    the turning point
                    the meditation of 'The always so'
                    The Now not followed by thought
                    the drift and dream
                    of being all and nothing
                    the effortless changing
                    that is timeless
                    even the body walking
                    as it does

(iii)

Many 'Buddhas' are seen,
but men and women
are driven to play with words:
many a 'Buddha' is distracted
by talking
believing, supposing and thinking.
Their name driven identity struggles
to interrupt The Only Buddha.

The mostly enlightened
hang on to their roles and responses:
they fear the silence of their new 'sight'
or the distress of their intimates
at their puzzling presentation.
They want to be kind and to help

    and so they act.

    may they still so act
   when they have given up
  belief in the talking puppet.

(iv)

It is windy
The sunlight
is coming in the West window
through an agitated camphor-laurel
Sunlight on spectacles
just happening
not followed
nothing
sunlight
and timeless it is
The Now contains it all
all of it Now

Development IX

'THE RELIEF GOES ON ...'

(i)

On the pier
"Give me two kilos of seagull cries —
sliced and wrapped —
'now'!" And finding "Now"?
A buffoon would have it thick or thin

(ii)

Of nothing is energy
it has direction
its own 'suchness'
it is Quality

(iii)

Work is some of that
but the direction of development
is inevitable
as the conviction of being an apprentice
was identity enough
a goose feather in place
being itself
The apprentice engages the world
He or she is learning to maintain clear sight
in the press of ordinary living and everyday suffering

(iv)

The shirt no longer fits
The joy
of no longer
struggling   trying   elaborating
is still there

(v)

the relief goes on
as if giving up an unpaid job as salesperson
for the 'I' that is not there
or giving up the job of stock-taker
in a cluttered warehouse
not required any more
While one hurts with every frightened child
suffering does not obstruct action.
The action is there when it is required
but not for its own sake
There are no sirens or flashing lights
And there is rest and repose
Such are the rewards
it is as well they cannot be conceived until experienced
or the limited zen centres would be overrun in the rush

(vi)

The children went down to Rocky Crossing
Twenty-five-year-old boots
one
then the other
on the Antarctic Beechleaf carpet
Lyre-bird does his repertoire from the right
some tops reflect a patch of sunlight
rarely a glimpse of blue
Winding down to side gullies
sweet water between the rocks
roughhewn log bridge
one step   next step

spinebill comes to have a look
fallen trees
covered with a fur of long green moss
lyre-bird scratchings
water tumbles over rocks somewhere ahead
Timeless 'Mu'
the cathedral of 'The always so'

Development IX

BUDDHAS AND BEAGLES

(i)

When early wrestling with a koan is becoming a part of experience, and then when kensho occurs, and later when seeing takes in more at a glance, but the sides of the mountain are not perceived, the koan is necessary, and sitting provides samadhi and personal experience of the Unity of Now.

(ii)

Knowing what is 'seen' may appear to have form, but as each form seems a natural aspect of the whole, the form doesn't matter, it is a glider flying with no fuel or propeller, only what it needs, and when there is no place to go, when it is already here, what does it need with wings or rudder, or form at all?

(iii)

One great student of the sutras was enlightened when he came indoors and his candle was blown out.

(iv)

The modes of experience
are immediately expressed
In a single breath
Joshu's "Wu!"

Total affirmation
One
call it   Mu   Eternity Nirvana   One
Immediate assertion of identity with All This
The struggling and suffering of Self taking action
Bodhisattva action
One and One   Identical   all in all
Joshu was on the balls of his feet with action

Buddhas and beagles
and in that same plosive exhalation
affirmation of the true nature
Of the Utterly One

Bodhisattva action is Nirvana

(v)

The fine branches rattle gum leaves in the wind
Mind over the illusory 'mind'
ecstatic emptiness, while 'the living altar'
is astride a planet in a spiral arm
and everything dances on an empty palm
when zazen 'ceases' nothing is different
It is still blown out
the missing hand, the finger cut off
and yet the dance continues   nothing —
every breath and every blink
all complete   totally One
Nothing! and yet —
the knuckles rap the table hard —
    Self

(vi)

'Nothing' cannot be called
Grasp for it and The Ten Thousand Things collide.
"Quiet. Sink from them,
leave the clutter that is not there."
The hall is empty
without effort: experience of peace is found
The plasma ocean glows
the breakers sound
the symphony growls its way around the curves
that are the nature of the hall
makes the ripples, shapes the waves
the singing rises and falls away
There are no words of fear
Form and time are dreamtime images ....
    to forget

Development IX

(vii)

Sitting here   there is no achievement
Timelessness is familiar
Explaining is abandoned
there are waves   and birds twittering
others being raucous   sometimes singing
Understanding is divested and then left alone
Effort is forgotten and concentration not required
Fish are breaking the surface
Even smiling is superfluous
Breathing and blinking are a pleasure
Complications are nowhere to be seen
There is no assertion required
It is tempting to stay with The Source
until the cries of children join the birdsong
and there are putrid bodies in the water
Working, Voice
    Jet engines roar

SHEEP TRACKS AND RABBIT DUNG

Sitting on close cropped grass
there are sheep tracks
and, to the right
rabbit dung on a small scraped mound
Breath is quiet; Winter sunshine is absorbed
Air is fresh; the light breeze cools an ear
Without thought The Eternal Face is heard
It has form and is formless, has no form and is not formless
the nature of 'The Way' is such
whether you say many words or be silent
if you 'see' or have the comfort of the blind
have merit or the destructive deeds of many lives
are said to have attained or failed
anonymous or found, empty of illusion
or counting The Ten Thousand Things

The Timeless Self holds it gently in The Hand
          enjoys breathing.

DEVELOPMENT X

Apprenticeship

(i)

Feeling is pivotal to the development of the apprentice: aware feeling, unclouded by thought or event, feeling now, quality projected effortlessly. Whatever 'sight' occurs is experienced through the maze of human process: 'concept sorter', 'eager word-smith', 'maps alive', whatever — coloured by such feeling.

Another view is that it is experienced despite all this 'human stuff' being in the way.

(ii)

There is wonder at the pain of humanity, as there is wonder at the beauty of the forest, wonder at the distress around the globe, wonder at the adaptation of many creatures, wonder at the numinous.

With those in distress there is quality in quiet deliverance, empathy too, but unless given leave, it is difficult to help. But being here can allow succour, even when it might sometimes be thought impossible.

(iii)

What patterns of gratification, habits of power, are together with the sight? The Jungians have been long aware of the unowned aspects of self. They gradually find acquaintance with denied aspects through self-awareness and therapy.

The shadow aspects long buried, the griefs, the wants, the hostility: are they well known and contained? Similarly, can self-importance preoccupations from later infancy be given up and the narcissistic cocoon of early development be opened?

The self may also be contaminated by infant struggles, not separate from an unnamed adversary.

Are such problems papered over, or have lessons been learned from the desire and frustration which is the developmental lot of men and women? The resolution of these issues of personal development forms the basis of 'character'.

(iv)

Without significant development of character, true seeing from the Buddha heart would be difficult indeed.

Can he or she face feelings right through the centre, and with new sight, transform this emotional energy to 'Heart': extend personal energy of the direct self?

This is loving action of breadth and simplicity.

And what of the effect of 'seeing' on the quality of the person? If the maturity of emotional and social development is as yet unfinished, will enlightenment itself shape the apprentice? Will real exposure to the suffering of others be containable?

Here: 'within' and 'without' are one: is that bearable?

(vi)

For the apprenticeship to be established, the transformation of 'the human spirit' gets under way. The 'seeing spirit' takes action, transforms the human drives, desires, and struggles to 'Heart'. The humanity does not expire but continues in full view, but the apprenticeship can still be sabotaged by the status keyed in, the power unrecognised, and desire unfulfilled.

(vii)

So the human self needs be known and harnessed for Right Action. The separate human organism is the vehicle for enlightenment. Shakyamuni expressed this many times: the human position on the wheel of life was the opportunity for deliverance.

(viii)

Awareness of both self and Universal Self is necessary. Wise application of the human self enables the 'View and the Humanity' to be one comfortably.

And the weave of personality? Credible? Worthy? Can it hold together appropriately? Be socially adaptable?

(ix)

Because 'sight' is from outside 'The Wheel of Life', time and 'The Ten Thousand Things', and because this 'seeing' is so comprehensive, there is a temptation to paralysis, to overvalue transcendence — stay there, to disengage from suffering and the action of the world.

This is like a man neglecting a pain in his chest.

And 'seeing' needs be full in any context: a crowd, in waking, with distraction, under contempt.

Because it is through 'sight', that feeling for hurt, despair and ignorance of the world becomes the driving force for engaged action.

(x)

It is only with the identity of what is seen and the 'heart' — feeling for it all, that seeing is 'seeing'. And the action — living it out, is beyond Enlightenment itself. Such loving action is the only true meaning of "gone beyond".

(xi)

But, at the brink:

This: unwanted by many because it is ordinary:

the true vision of personal insignificance.

Ordinary

(i)

The 'seeing' experience gives the better view of what 'ordinary' is. This bit is about 'ordinary' being the subject of kensho — intimately and only being ordinary with every leaf and breeze. 'Not I' has no wish to attract attention, but will engage whenever required. To smile is ordinary, stepping aside, waiting, walking — 'ordinary' is unobtrusive contentment.

(ii)

Ordinary walking is wind, grass and raindrops — children's voices and smoker's coughs — not other. Ordinary experience is a Bosnian village under shellfire as much as Oponohu Bay, includes petty frustration and indifference as well as acceptance, nurture and interest. In contrast to the usual view, the experience is not subjective, not dual, but experienced as Self.

(iii)

Certainly not idyllic — the 'opposites' are not granted form, but ordinary man's viewpoint is fully felt, a mixture of insecurity and contentment, pain and satisfaction.

(iv)

Aware that this planet in the Twentieth Century appears as it does only from the human viewpoint, by this type of brain process, this experience of 'time'.

(v)

The Anthropic Principle's implications (science version) are only at the earliest stage of being addressed. However it will be through such views that 'ordinary' is 'seen' in scale.

Joshu's humour and Nansen's sword

(i)

Zen developed to a model of rapid enlightenment — enlightenment in one lifetime. It contrasts with other schools of Buddhism in that respect. This is purposeful intent. And because it is possible, to be of value it needs to be balanced with the human character and the resources of the person who is its vehicle.

(ii)

Zen is to be tested: wishful dualists want petty compromise, some the decade's vogue, some the unchanging rigours of great monasteries, while others would establish ignorance or lose the dharma to religiosity.

'Seeing' will be tested more: some 'see' truly, but stop striving to 'see' further, and their lives are not transformed by their 'sight'.

Nansen, Joshu and Hui-nêng will meet them face to face: "From the beginning not a thing is." But there is Joshu's humour and Nansen's sword. They will test such men and women hard. To become a journeyman is to be tested by the minute.

(iii)

Considering the impetus for 'seeing', it is inevitable that many will develop insight and substantial enlightenment. But without awareness of personal insignificance, they will not know how far they must carry their vision.

The student after great effort passes his final exams, only to see that he must learn the actions of his trade — exemplify by what he does and the quality imbued in it, and, that the examination, while a requirement for this, in no way does away with any aspect of the learning and practice of every action required.

(iv)

And each time there is a surge of 'seeing': all there at once, the apprentice laughs at what he thought he saw the last time this happened, until he knows it will happen again ... and again ... and submits.

(v)

There is indeed far to go from the first koan shock: the intuitive enlightenment is as worthless as the morning star on a very foggy morning without the identity, the 'Heart', and the ability to go back to the market place without 'I', and do that in a manner experienced well by others, but being ordinary, doesn't draw undue attention.

(vi)

'Seeing' and 'not-seeing', 'development' and 'no development': dreamtime play — there is only action.

The Waves in Che-chiang

(i)

I go to work. That does not mean 'I' of course. Whatever the 'seeing', going about everyday business: eating, walking, loving is what happens. The verse by Su Tung-p'o that is traditionally used to describe this is best included.

> Misty rain on Mount Lu
> and waves in Che-chiang
> When you have not been there,
> Many a regret surely you have;
>
> But once there and homeward you wend,
> How Matter-of-fact things look!
> Misty rain on Mount Lu,
> And waves surging in Che-chiang.

(ii)

Those with hope and distress, still come forward and 'work' is done. If face to face teaching is not inevitable, then koan wrestling can be sidelined, and the habits of the student mind however joyful are relinquished, allowing energy to flow into day to day practice.

The long-held 'I' habits — give way gradually, as Now/dhyana/Reality/Mind moves as it moves. The self marshals words to the task of communicating what is. Even 'I's neurotic habits, such as retreating to reading, being a professional eldest child and wanting to be heard, are turned to advantage.

THE ENDORPHINS OF CONTENTMENT

(i)

'Not wanting' is rewarding. The outgoing loving of others is made easy. The body functions as is its nature. Harmony and good feelings are the usual experience. The endorphins of contentment are more reliable than any from the poppy or test-tube. And, once experienced, it would be difficult to return to rebuilding the imagined attributes and the wants of 'I'.

(ii)

Paying attention to 'suchness': plants and people, skinks and flowers, sky and sea: is so rewarding that there is little time or need for delusion.

(iii)

In literature, dreams inspire, imagination is rich, the very matrix of creativity, and this is particularly enjoyed if there is a keen awareness of illusion/delusion. So too with everyday living. Seeing from the true nature of self and being free from 'ignorance' is 'the way' (that is, 'free' in the sense of 'not fooled by or oppressed by'). In other words, you look for 'The Kingdom' within the self — but what a Self!

(iv)

When dhyana is all there is, dhyana is experienced in all activities. Out in the world this 'nothing special zen' happens while struggling with the elements of apprenticeship.

(v)

To be apprenticed to The Sound is to let It develop — as zazen sharpens awareness, does not turn away from any of it.

Yet to be The Sound and not know more than a small part of The Sound is inevitable, to be limited is inevitable, that is why there is a clear identity, but an apprenticeship just the same.

LIMITATION

(i)

There is even more limitation in being a social animal, with a social field and all the habits of its culture as well as the social animal's individual and family development.

But the characteristics of the singular human: to be curious, to complete what is part known, explain the changed perception, to channel the emotional states of the organism, are such as to provide the energy, for they are strength of 'The always so'.

(ii)

For ultimately the development of practical wisdom from such sources nourishes the capacity for giving. Wisdom derived from 'seeing', must be contained, adapted, plied to the world's needs. It is heart and hands wisdom which is required — wisdom in action — to benefit the globe's creatures, yet usable because it is ordinary and matter of fact.

(iii)

The apprentice will not be in a hurry, will let others take the leading role, will wait while the young trial and learn, will give his or her skills freely and encourage their use. And not give up — at the seeming impasse, the push will always be strong enough.

(iv)

As well as compassion for pain, as well as comfort of the defensive and the insecure, there needs to develop a lucid sense of The Middle Way in 'Now' without benefit of written principles, but a Way with flow to quality as water flows to the valley.

The principles of dynamic Oneness allow uninhibited kindness: when known it is unstoppable.

THE FULL CIRCLE

(i)

During zen development much effort and concentration must go into awareness of the nature of 'self'. From this there is the awareness of the basic oneness of all selves, as if a full circle has been travelled and there is the knowing that every trusting child has anyway.

(ii)

While this is a religious theme, and beginning an apprenticeship in such a direction cannot be anything else, it is not an acceptance of religiosity.

The ritual affirmation of the nature of Self is natural and sustaining, and the shared expression of similar religious feeling can even revitalise a community when facing stress and despair. Such affirmation will have countless forms: and, if the form does not distract from the essence or create "Us and Them" divisions, the community will thrive in the greater world. Each form might be lived, but the apprentice does not abide with any form.

(iii)

Yet he or she knows those who share the planet as neighbours as well as self, so acts accordingly — the example grows in many, speaks gently, sensitive to the verge of hurt where men and women fall too easily. Gentle speech is positive: the frame and the picture are both accepted when kindness has wrought them.

But The Emperor of China could not hold Bodhidharma at the Court: he went away to do what was required.

(iv)

Although the apprentice might take the precepts through The Middle Way, the presence of a different quality is there: his and her identity illuminates the market place. Without boundaries 'Not I' smiles the assurance beyond birth and death, holds and heals those members caught in fear and the pain of 'want'.

And he or she goes on, not because of a literal vow, but simply because the spreading awareness of shared Buddha-nature is the natural development.

Partnership

(i)

In submission to 'Not I' and the falling away from The Ten Thousand Things, the self engaging the world does not stand alone. Know that Self is one and many who have goals in common. Trust is easily put in the right direction.

Loving cooperation comes naturally in meeting the 'other' self who strives to 'see', or from whom Self shines through consciously or otherwise. Such joining has immense strength for development and loving action.

(ii)

Teilhard had the vision of this Christic element spreading in humanity. It is Buber's sense of human reality extant in its consummate form, Rumi's overwhelming experience of his teacher Sham's presence, Dante's union with Beatrice.

Returning to the market place, the puissance of such twosomes or groups might channel unprecedented energy to growth of the family, other apprentices, the society and the world.

(iii)

It is a challenge to Zen that is already being taken up: the teachers, the sangha, to take 'Bodhisattva action' to their societies, to have a need for a word like 'compassioning' to describe the doing that develops with Zen leadership.

China and Japan honed, purified and maintained the enlightened view. But as kensho follows kensho — this 'sight' can only leave the sitting hall, encompass social engagement, action, development.

The author sat up straight when an Australian radio journalist reporting on the early aftermath of the Kobe earthquake, said, "There was even a 'right wing organisation' all dressed in black (who came to help)".

The Zen Buddhist monks' traditional dress is not readily known in Western society.

(iv)

This active engagement will be done by a 'Society within society' whose tools will be kind action, good example, brave succour, which will happen where it is most required. Whatever the strengths of its 'sitting' and 'seeing' there will be no elite concerns or behaviours. They are irrelevant to those with arrow wounds and emphysema, or suffer from alienation and oppression.

(v)

There will be co-operative work of the Utterly One. It might be alongside mullah and pastor, priest and rabbi, wherever development leads.

The Utterly One has many names and it does not matter in whose name kindness occurs. There are many helpful actions, much comfort to give, pain to share, and this is so ... fullstop.

This enhanced growth as a result of cooperative accomplishment is optimum when 'Not I' is unquestionable. 'Not-I' is working with Itself.

("ALL THIS ZEN TALK")

(i)

What all this zen talk amounts to, is going about everyday business, doing what must be done, with elements of samadhi integrated with elements of skill, balancing elements of foolishness and the forgetting of one's identity with ever developing knowledge of who it is who moves and writes and talks. At the supermarket or the workplace, ultimately the news of 'the gate' must show upon the face.

This portion of humanity goes back to the family, the fruit trees, watches magnolias grow, reads Phillip Adams in the weekend papers, and works in the market place.

Know your face.

Development X

Glossary

Expressions in English which have a more comprehensive meaning in this text.

'All this'
See 'Just this' and 'All this' on the next page.

Always So (The) or 'The always so'
IT he Utterly One', Self, Universal Self, 'The Sound', 'The Unborn', (see page 145 for some of the many synonyms) — but with the particular Implication of timelessness. Also 'timeless suchness'.

'apprentice'
One who is learning to adapt 'sightfult living to This which is Utterly One.

'Bodhisattva action'
Moral and compassionate action, free as a result of 'seeing', and essentially seeking broad good outcome. The action to which the apprentice aspires. See bodhisattva entry on p 240. The expression implies that there is only the action and thus no such being as a Bodhisattva.

'Buddha nature'
The nature of any process as part of the One Process.

'emptiness'
A state which is neither 'being' nor 'non-being'. It implies Self living fully energetic, open, immediate. It also implies in the moment complementarity between being and non-being'.

'everything' or 'The Everything'
Used in the text to approximate the thinking of the man or woman in the street in thinking about 'The always so'. The suffix 'thing' and the implication of absolute pantheism makes it an unsuitable and confusing word to convey Buddhist insight.

'gestalt'
A word in psychology literature long borrowed from the German Language and refers to a pattern of experience. It implies that the whole is experienced at once and also implies that elements may be perceived as 'foreground' or 'background'. It is a pivotal word to understand parallel processing by the brain and its implications.

'the goose'
When italicised refers to the koan *'The goose is out'* In capitals it is another synonym for 'The Sound'.

Heart
The sensibility of feeling Now, transformed to action of Self. Identity beliefs and other knowledge schemata about the individual, and the motivations and behaviours that are sourced from these.

'ignorance'
Refers to states of mind when prajna is not realised, particularly when there are dualistic preoccupations. Prajna is a Sanskrit word meaning 'enlightened wisdom'. Looked at more definitively it implies a true awareness of Itself by 'Not I'.

'Just this'
an awareness of a simple truth about the nature of self, met directly in zazen — "and there is nothing else"

'All this'
Seeing that the 'just this' truth is universal and consistent.
As the brain has a broad capacity to integrate perception, memory and anticipation, let alone have dimensions subsumed under 'sensibility', there is the illusion that 'just this' and lall this' are different in essence. The illusion is compounded because of many parallel and confusing functions of the nervous system. (Zazen simplifies these.) *"Zen is your every day mind."*

'knocker'
Australian colloquialism.
Macquarie Dictionary: 'A persistently hostile critic or carping detractor'.
It has other meanings, but this is the meaning in the text.

malarky
Macquarie Dictionary: 'nonsense, meaningless talk'

'Mind'
capital 'M' (See 'Now' and 'Reality')
The immediate experience of brain process. There are implications of Mind with a capital 'M'. One is 'Mind/ Universal Self'. Second: there is no such thing as 'a mind': it is not something that 'I' possesses. Third: it is Process.

'no boundaries'
Refers to the arbitrary nature of boundaries and freedom from subject/ object social prescriptions.

'Not 1'
When the 'I' illusion is penetrated, 'seen' for what it is and put in its place, and the experience without boundaries continues, then 'Not I' is an attempt to express it in words.

'Now' : Capital 'N' (See also 'Mind' and 'Reality')
The immediate experience of brain process.

pia mater (Latin, used in English as an anatomical term) The inner membrane covering the brain .

'Reality' capital 'R' (See 'Now' and 'Mind')
The immediate experience of brain process.

'seeing' (also other forms of the verb 'so see')
Used with inverted commas and refers to perception incorporating an enlightened viewpoint. It implies persistent and consistent 'seeing'.

'self'
The integrated processes of the nervous system Now. see p73
(Note: 'self' is not used in these pages to refer to identity beliefs or other knowledge schemata about the individual, including false self processes described in self-psychology; as such its usage is in contradistinction to 'I'. It is yet an integrate of the five skandas which Shakyamuni saw had no substance. In psychotherapy a well functioning 'self' is generally a good outcome.)

Self
'Not I' as Universal Self.

'sightful'
adj. as for seeing' above.

'the five skandas'
perception, intuition, sensation, thinking and feeling: Sixth Century BC, but fairly accurate view of the neuro-physiological processes.

'skink'
smooth scaled lizard constituting the family Scincidae.

'suchness'
inherent quality.

Suchness
It processes as it processes, it moves as it moves, totally one, incredibly complex — it is me the cookie that crumbles, but when really known; all crumbling and no cookie. In Sanskrit - tathata.

'the suchness of The Always So'
This is more self explanatory.

'The Sound'
An abbreviation for 'the sound of one hand clapping', but it is synonymous with the many other terms for Universal Self.

'The Unborn'
Shakyamuni's expression for 'The always so' and all the other synonyms for Self.

timelessness
See explanation in 'The Inevitable Koan' - pp 139-145

'Utter Oneness'
Means just that. It implies no duality in any dimension.

'wishful thinking'
This term has a usage wider than usual. It implies wishes for duality: that there are breaks, discontinuities, inconsistencies in the Utterly One.

Words used other than English

Sanskrit

Atman	ambiguous term: it has usage as 'the individual soul' who survives from life to life, but from an enlightened point of view: Universal Self. see p 166
bodhi	the truth' in an enlightened sense
bodhisattva	In legend, an enlightened saint who has transcended 'the wheel of life', but who chooses to return and save the beings of the world. While this might be an inference from consistent Bodhisattva action, there is an implication of separateness in the appellation. In this volume the notion of 'Bodhisattva action' is preferred.

Buddha	'enlightened one'
dharma	The law or teaching: it implies the true teaching and imparting of 'sight'. See p 89
dhyana	Meditation
karma	fate, or better 'the action of the world', but the word has taken on many and contradictory meanings see pages 90-91 and 182
nirvana	'Eternal transcendent state'
prajna	The wisdom of 'sight', or similarly enlightened wisdom (see under ignorance')
sangha	A particular Buddhist community. (with sight' it has a much wider implication)
samadhi	Special mental state of high quality achieved during meditation
samsara	The moving wheel of birth, death and rebirth.
Shakyamuni	means 'sage of the Shakya people' and refers to Siddhartha Gautama — the Buddha. More correctly rendered without the 'h' and with diacritic marks over the 'S' and first 'a'.
Sunyatta	Nothingness or Emptiness
Sutra	Buddhist sacred scripture
Tathagata (The)	The 'Thus Come' see p 182

Chinese

wu	'No' or 'Nothing'.
ch' an	Meditation, comparable to dhyana in Sanskrit and *zen* in Japanese.

Japanese

mu	'Not or 'Nothing' When rendered with a capital 'M', it refers to the seeing experience attained after sitting practice and study of Joshu's famous koan with a Zen master.
kensho	Sudden insight
koan (pl. koan)	short paradoxical statement or story used in zen training. See pages 36 to 37 and 59 to 61
sassho	turning questions about a koan asked to enhance enlightenment
satori	sudden and comprehensive enlightenment
sesshin	special assembly of the sangha for meditation and development.
teisho	showing a teaching to pupils. Perhaps better is: 'a graphically demonstrated teaching'
zazen	sitting meditation
shikan taza	simple meditation

List of books: including some mentioned in the text and other books of particular interest.

Aitken R. *Taking the Path of Zen,* North Point Press San Francisco

Aitken R. *The Mind of Clover,* Essays in Zen Buddhist Ethics North Point Press San Francisco

Aitken R. and Steindl-Rast D. *The Ground we Share,* **Nelson Foster** Ed. Triumph Books

Aitken R. *The Practice of Perfection The Paramitas from a Zen Buddhist Perspective,* Pantheon Books

Aitken R. *Encouraging Words,* Pantheon

Aitken R. *The Dragon who never sleeps,* Parallax Press Berkeley California

Arasteh A.R. *Rumi the Persian, the Sufi,* Routledge and Kegan Paul

Beck Joko C. *Everyday Zen,* **Steve Smith** Ed Harper San Francisco

Bion W.R. *Experiences in Groups,* Tavistock Publications

Blyth R.H. *Writings in Games Zen Masters Play,* **Sohi R. & Carr A.** Eds Mentor

Bowlby J. *Attachment and Loss,* (in three volumes) The Hogarth Press and Penguin

Byles M.B. *Footprints of Gautama The Buddha,* A Quest book.

Doctorow E.L *Loon Lake,* Macmillan

Dogen E. *Moon in a Dewdrop,* **Kazuaki Tanahashi** Ed. Element Books

Engel G. L. *Anxiety and Depression-Withdrawal: The Primary Affects of Unpleasure.* The International Journal of Psychoanalysis 1962 Parts 2-3 Volume 43

Erikson E.H. *Childhood and Society,* Revised Edition Penguin Books

Herrigal E. *Zen and the Art of Archery,* Translated by **R.F.C. Hull** Forward by **D.T.Suzuki** Routledge and Kegan Paul

Humphries C. *Buddhism An introduction and guide*, Penguin

Horney K. *Neurosis and Human Growth*, Norton

Imbach J.D. *The Recovery of Love*, Crossroad New York

Jacques E. *Death and The Mid-life Crisis*, International Journal Psychoanalysis (1965) 46: 502-514.

Jung C.G. Foreword in Suzuki's *'Introduction to Zen Buddhism'*

Kadowaki J.K SJ *Zen and the Bible*, translated from the Japanese by **Joan Rieck** Arkana

Kelly G.A. *A Theory of Personality*, The Norton Library

Kersten H. *Jesus lived in India,* Element

Klien M. *Envy and Gratitude,* Delta

Kornfield J. *A Path with Heart A guide through the perils and promises of spiritual life,* Bantam Trade Paperback

Küng H. *Does God Exist?* Collins

Küng H. , van Ess J. , von Stietencron H. & Bechert H. *Christianity and the World Religions,* Translated by **P. Heinegg** Collins

Lin Y utang Ed. *The Wisdom of China,* New English Library Four Square

Matthiessen P. *Nine-headed Dragon River,* Shambala Boston

Merton T. *Thomas Merton on Zen,* Sheldon Press London (Includes *Zen and the Birds of Appetite* which is now published separately by Shambala)

Pirsig R. *Zen and the Art of Motor Cycle Maintenance*, The Bodley Head & Corgi

Rogers Carl R. *On Becoming a Person* Constable

Schloegl Irmgard *The Zen Way* Sheldon Press

Schloegl Irmgard *The Wisdom of the Zen Masters,* New Directions

Paperback

S**uttie Ian D.** *The Origins of Love and Hate,* Foreword by **John Bowlby** Free Association Books

Suzuki Daisetz Teitaro *Studies in Zen,* Unwin Hyman Limited

Suzuki Daisetz Teitaro *Zen Buddhism,* **William Barret**t Ed Doubleday Anchor Book

Suzuki Daisetz Teitaro *Essays in Zen Buddhism First Series (also Second Series and Third Series),* Rider

Suzuki Daisetz Teitaro *Introduction to Zen Buddhism,* includes Foreword by **C.G. Jung** Rider

Suzuki Daisetz Teitaro *The Zen Doctrine of No Mind,* Rider

Suzuki Daisetz Teitaro *The Awakening of Zen,* **Christmas Humphries** Ed Shambala Dragon Editions

Suzuki Daisetz Teitaro *Manual of Zen Buddhism,* Rider

Teilhard de Chardin P. *The Phenomenon of Man,* Collins

Teilhard de Chardin P. *Le Milieu Divin,* Fontana

Teilhard de Chardin P. *Hymn of the Universe,* Collins

Undset Sigrid *Kristin Lavransdatter,* translated by **Charles Archer and J.S.Scott** Cassell

Vidal Gore *Creation,* Granada Paperback

A Buddhist Bible, **Dwight Goddard** Ed. 1970 Edition Beacon Press

Bhagavad Gita, translation by S**wami Swarupananda** published by Advaita Ashrama Calcutta Penguin, Arkana edition: translation and introduction by **Eknath Easwaran**

Jerusalem Bible, Doubleday N.Y.

King James Bible, Cambridge University Press

Dhammapada, translated by **The Venerable Balangoda Ananda Maitreya** Revised by **Rose Kramer** Lotsawa

The Gospel According to Thomas, rendered by **Pico Iyer Raghavan Iyer** Ed. Concord Grove Press

Khayyam Omar *The Rubaiyat of Omar Khayam,* done into English by **Edward Fitzgerald** (numerous publishers)

The Upanishads, translated by **Swami Prabhavananda and F. Manchester** Vedanta Press

Tao te Ching, **'Lao Tzu'** Concord Grove Press

The Wu-men Kuan (Mumonkan) The Gateless Barrier, **Aitken R.** Trans. Commentary by **Aitken R.**

www.ingramcontent.com/pod-product-compliance
Lightning Source LLC
Chambersburg PA
CBHW051540010526
44107CB00064B/2802